LETTER TO THE SPANISH AMERICANS

LETTRE

AUX

ESPAGNOLS-AMÉRICAINS.

PAR

UN DE LEURS COMPATRIOTES.

Vincet Amor Patriæ.
" L'Amour de la Patrie l'emportera."

A PHILADELPHIE.

MDCCXCIX.

1799.

Juan Pablo Viscardo y Guzmán

LETTER
TO THE
SPANISH
AMERICANS

A facsimile of the
second English edition
(London, 1810)

With an Introduction by
D. A. Brading

The John Carter Brown Library
Providence, Rhode Island

Published with the assistance of
The Center for New World Comparative Studies
at the John Carter Brown Library

ISBN 0-916617-58-0

The John Carter Brown Library is an independently
funded and administered institution for advanced research
in history and the humanities, located at Brown University
since 1901. The Library houses one of the world's outstanding
collections of books, maps, and manuscripts relating to
the colonial period of the Americas, North and South,
from 1492 to ca. 1825.

Correspondence should be directed to the

John Carter Brown Library
Box 1894
Providence, Rhode Island 02912
or to *JCBL_Publications@brown.edu*
Additional information may be found at *www.JCBL.org.*

Frontispiece: Title page of the earliest printed edition of
Viscardo y Guzmán's letter, which first appeared in the French
language. The imprint "A Philadelphie" is probably false. The volume
was almost certainly printed and published in London.

CONTENTS

PREFACE

IT WOULD BE HARD TO SAY whether the purpose of this little book is more to honor the long-forgotten Juan Pablo Viscardo y Guzmán (d. 1798) or the much heralded David Brading, for many years director of the Centre for Latin American Studies at Cambridge University and still quite among the living. In fact, the purpose is to do both.

Viscardo y Guzmán's "Letter to the Spanish Americans" was a spur to action comparable, in some respects, to Thomas Paine's "Common Sense" in the United States in 1776. In Peru and elsewhere today, after many years of neglect, Viscardo is celebrated as a great forerunner of the movement for political independence in colonial Spanish America. Like Paine, he was able to concentrate thinking and focus the discontent among the American-born Spaniards, i.e., the so-called "creoles," as distinguished from the native peoples (the Amerindians), and the *"peninsulares,"* the Spaniards temporarily living in Spanish America, often with considerable privilege.

In British America, only a generation before, the discontent was similar. George Washington and Benjamin Franklin both were deeply resentful of the preferment given in America to mediocre British-born subjects of the crown in contrast to highly talented American-born subjects. Among the most powerful motives behind Washington's and Franklin's subscription to the revolutionary cause was precisely that problem.

It is one of the missions of this Library to promote the comparative study of the diverse societies, cultures, and governments in the New World, across the conventional boundaries. This publication serves that end. It may even be looked upon as a sequel to another small book published by the Library a few years ago, *Do the Americas Have a Common History?/ ¿Tienen las Américas una Historia Comun?* (1998) by Sir J. H. Elliott.

Professor Brading was the Andrew W. Mellon Senior Research Fellow at the John Carter Brown Library for five months in the fall of 2000, and among his many contributions to the community of scholars at the jcb, and to the Brown University campus in general, was a lecture he gave on Viscardo. It was obvious there was a vast gap between the celebration of Viscardo in Spanish America and the near complete ignorance of his name in the United States. It seemed to us mandatory that we try to close that gap a little by this publication, with Professor Brading's insightful introduction and a contemporary translation into English of Viscardo's address. Professor Brading cheered on this project because he felt that the book would be useful in courses on colonial Latin America in English-speaking colleges and universities.

It was no little incentive to us, as well, that with the Maury A. Bromsen-Simón Bolívar Room now beautifully installed in the Library, all aspects of the revolutions for independence in South America have taken on added interest here.

Given Professor Brading's stature as a historian, the Library feels privileged to have his name permanently associated with this institution in a publication. Professor Brading is the author of *The First America: The Spanish Monarchy, Creole Patriots, and the Liberal State, 1492–1867* (1991) and numerous other books, including most recently, *Church and State in Bourbon Mexico. The Diocese of Michoacan, 1749–1810* (1994) and *Mexican Phoenix: Our Lady of Guadalupe. Image and Tradition across Five Centuries* (2001). All of his books are routinely translated into Spanish, and he has received numerous honors from governments and institutions of higher learning in Mexico and South America. He was director of the Centre for Latin American Studies at Cambridge from 1975 to 1990, and in 1995 he was elected a Fellow of the British Academy.

The publication history of Viscardo y Guzmán's "Letter" is complex. Dr. Burton Van Name Edwards, Principal Cataloguer at the JCB, has sorted out the facts in a bibliographical note at the end of this volume.

NORMAN FIERING
Director and Librarian
John Carter Brown Library

INTRODUCTION

by D. A. Brading

JUAN PABLO VISCARDO Y GUZMÁN
CREOLE PATRIOT AND *PHILOSOPHE*

I

On 10 February 1798, Rufus King, the American minister in London, recorded the death of Juan Pablo Viscardo y Guzmán (1748–98), a former Peruvian Jesuit, whom he had known by the pseudonym of Paoli Rossi. In his journal he noted that he had visited Viscardo the day before and that the dying man had entrusted him with "a parcel of papers," accompanied by "a request that I would have it published for his credit and the happiness of mankind." The next day he had returned to the Jesuit's lodgings in New Road, Marylebone, only to find him very ill, able to utter but a few incoherent phrases about the revolution in South America and to say how little he trusted Francisco de Miranda, the Venezuelan patriot.

King recalled that he had first met Viscardo at the close of 1796 when the Peruvian had confided that although he was a paid agent of the British Foreign Office, he now suspected that its ministers were planning to have him assassinated. He had enquired about the possibility of emigrating to Philadelphia and had asked King to take care of his papers and some £400 or £500 in cash for investment in American bonds.[1] But the American had succeeded in allaying his fears and encouraged him to visit Downing Street, where, as it turned out, he was welcomed and promptly received payment of his outstanding stipend.

If King took such an interest in Viscardo, it was in part because he was a leading Federalist politician and a staunch foe of the French Revolution. In particular, he hoped to mount an Anglo-American intervention in Spanish America so as to secure its independence, since "if it is not assisted

3

by England, the work will be done by France, who will introduce there her detestable principles, divide it into small Republics, put bad men at their head, and by these means facilitate her meditated Enterprises against us." It was with this aim in mind that King established cordial relations with Francisco de Miranda, who had recently arrived in London disillusioned with the course of events in France and hopeful of obtaining British support.[2] By way of assistance, King gave Miranda Viscardo's "parcel of papers," and with an unerring eye, the Venezuelan selected and in 1799 published the Jesuit's *Lettre aux Espagnols-Américains,* a paper printed in London, but with the false imprint of Philadelphia. Two years later he sponsored a Spanish translation of the work, also published in London and entitled *Carta derijada a los Españoles Americanos.* Moreover, in 1806, when Miranda finally succeeded in landing in Venezuela at the head of a small expedition, he distributed copies of this inflammatory pamphlet. Two years later, when Miranda sponsored the publication of a collection of documents in part dealing with his expedition, he included as an appendix an English translation of Viscardo's *Letter,* since he was persuaded that "this little treatise had more between its covers...than all the speeches and assertions about Spain and South America."[3] Such was the impression created in London by Viscardo's manifesto in favour of independence, that in 1809 James Mill gave an account of it in *The Edinburgh Review,* where he asserted that the Peruvian Jesuit had "left behind him various manuscripts on the state of his country which we have reason to believe were highly worthy of seeing the light."[4]

Despite this flurry of interest in Great Britain, in Peru the prolongation of the wars of independence until 1824 consigned Viscardo and his work into oblivion. In his ample *Diccionario histórico-biográfico del Perú* (1874–90), Manuel de Mendiburu omitted all reference to the Jesuit.[5] In effect, it was not until the twentieth century that the *Letter* was re-published and research into Viscardo's background and career began. This work of historical recuperation was primarily undertaken by two Jesuit scholars, Rubén Vargas Ugarte of Peru and the Catalan, Miguel Batllori.[6] However, it was left to an American historian, Merle E. Simmons, to discover that Miranda had ultimately returned Viscardo's "parcel of papers" to Rufus King and that together with all King's papers it had been deposited in the library of the New-York Historical Society. In 1983 a transcription of all Viscardo's manuscripts was published in Caracas in their original French, and thereafter the manuscripts were translated into Spanish and published in Lima. Simmons later located other copies of these manuscripts in the papers of Sir James Bland Burges, Viscardo's protector in the Foreign Office, which had been deposited in the Bodleian Library at Oxford.[7] It is thanks to the discovery and publication of Viscardo's complete works that it is now possible to trace his remarkable intellectual trajectory and to demonstrate the profound changes in his thinking wrought by his residence in London.

II

It was in 1781 that a Peruvian exile in Italy addressed a series of four letters to John Udney, the British consul at Leghorn, in which he announced that a descendant of the Incas, one Tupac Amaru, the cacique of Tinta, had recently launched a rebellion "to liberate the Indians from the slavery of Spain and to recover the empire of his ancestors." Letters had arrived from South America which averred that the uprising had engulfed the entire highland region of the Peruvian viceroyalty and that separate movements had appeared in Charcas and Quito. Citing the news that a British naval expedition with 3,000 soldiers on board was about to enter the River Plate, the exile urged the consul to recommend to his superiors the capture of the port of Buenos Aires, assuring him that the invaders would meet with no resistance. For his part, he offered his services to the British Government, emphasizing that, although he had left Peru in 1768 when aged twenty, he had been raised in the province of Arequipa and had studied for seven years in the city of Cuzco, the only place where "a true idea of Peru" could be obtained. The son of a family blessed with landed estates, he could speak "Peruvian," which was to say, Quechua, not to mention French and Italian, and thus was eminently qualified to assist the British in any attempt to liberate his homeland.[8]

If this former Jesuit approached Udney, it was because he was convinced that "the mutual mistrust" of the races which inhabited Peru had been superseded by their ever-mounting hatred of the colonial regime and its countless tyrannies. In particular, the American Spaniards bitterly resented their exclusion from high office in Church and State since, although their forefathers had conquered Peru at the expense of "their blood and sweat," their homeland was now governed by European Spaniards who derided their very claims to nobility. And yet, until now, it had been a point of honour for the creoles, as Spaniards born in the New World were called, to sustain the authority of their sovereign over the Indians and mestizos. In any case, both the mestizos and mulattos saw themselves as an extension of the hispanic class and respected the creoles as their natural leaders. As regards the Indians, it should be recalled that most creoles had suckled the milk of their

Indian nurses; all their houses supported a numerous group of Indian servants; and as priests the creoles defended the natives from the oppression of their European magistrates. After two-and-a-half centuries of residence in the New World, the American Spaniards had been "converted into almost the same people" as the mestizos and Indians. By way of conclusion, the exile reminded the consul that, with seven million inhabitants, Peru would constitute a rich market for British merchandise, especially since under Spain all imported goods sold for three to four times their value in Europe.[9]

If Juan Pablo Viscardo y Guzmán offered his services to the British government, it was because he himself was a victim of Spanish despotism. In Cuzco both he and his brother, José Anselmo, had taken their first vows as Jesuits while still adolescents and were thus suddenly consigned to a penurious exile when, in 1767, Charles III decreed the summary expulsion of all Jesuits from the far-flung territories of the Spanish monarchy. On arrival in Italy the two young men, who had yet to receive the tonsure, left the Company of Jesus and thus became mere laymen, supported only by a royal pension of eighteen pesos, twelve reales a year, at that time barely more than the wage of an inferior servant.

In these circumstances it was only to be expected that the two brothers placed all their hopes on obtaining their shares of the estates left by their parents and an uncle who had entered the priesthood. Born and bred in Pampacolca in the valley of Majes, the two exiles descended from Juan Viscardo y Guzmán, a Spaniard who had settled in the region in about 1630. His son, their grandfather, married an heiress of Pampacolca and acted as lieutenant of the corregidor of Condesuyos. Like many provincial landowners in the Andean highlands, the family was linked by marriage to a lineage of Indian *kurakas*. As was equally common, the wealth of the family estates barely sufficed to maintain all its children, so that among their uncles and aunts they counted two priests and two nuns. For all that, their father left an estate worth 52,000 pesos in 1765 and their uncle an amount somewhat greater. However, although the two exiles persistently petitioned the Spanish crown both to return to Peru and for a judicial settlement of their inheritance, they never received any satisfaction, albeit in large measure because their three married sisters had divided the estate between them and took no interest in the fate of their brothers.[10] In effect, Juan Pablo Viscardo y Guzmán was a provincial gentleman who spent almost two decades in Italy hoping and scheming to recover his birthright, all the while growing ever more resentful of the Spanish government which had expelled him from his homeland.

From June 1782 to March 1784, Viscardo and his brother stayed in London where they received a small subvention from the Foreign Office. In October 1782 he addressed a letter to the British Government, urging the immediate despatch of a naval expedition to South America, offering his hosts the great prize, "the conquest of Buenos Aires," a thriving port which was so isolated from the provinces it governed that its inhabitants could offer little resistance. At a time when Britain was about to lose the Thirteen Colonies, this acquisition would provide lands for the North American loyalists. It could also serve as a base of operation both for the destruction of the Spanish fleet and for an expedition on land to invade Peru and thus re-establish "the throne of the Incas." All hopes that this intriguing operation might be launched were thwarted by changes in the British government and the peace treaty signed between Spain and Great Britain in 1783. By then news had reached London of the collapse of the 1780 rebellion and the execution of its leaders. With their services no longer required, the two brothers returned to Italy, where José Anselmo soon died, leaving an impoverished widow and a young daughter.[11]

Back in Italy, in July 1784, Viscardo wrote to the British consul at Genoa, Evan Nepean, informing him that recent letters from Peru had stated that the bishop of Cuzco, Juan Manuel Moscoso y Peralta, together with his dean, two canons, and sixteen parish priests, had been arrested and were now confined in Lima, awaiting their despatch to Spain. Although Moscoso had valiantly defended Cuzco from Tupac Amaru's forces, raising a regiment of clerics, he had been subsequently accused of treasonable correspondence with the rebel leader. But why had the rebellion failed? In Viscardo's opinion, Tupac Amaru's pretensions to the Inca throne had mortally offended the pride of the creole nobility since, "owing to their great contempt for the Indians, the creoles were not disposed to accept one of them as their master." Moreover, the rebel leader in Charcas had massacred many American Spaniards. At the same time, the Inca lineages of Cuzco all rejected Tupac Amaru's claims to ancestral authority. The result was that creole military leaders were able to draw upon considerable Indian support when they advanced against the rebels. In effect, Viscardo here openly admitted that "the mutual distrust" of the races which inhabited Peru had destroyed the possibility of mounting a common action against the colonial regime.[12]

In the years that followed, Viscardo corresponded both with Antonio Porlier, the new Spanish Minister of the

Indies, about his inheritance, and with Sir John Acton, the formidable prime minister of the kingdom of Naples, about a commercial treaty with Spain. He was by then employed as secretary or vice-consul of the Marquis of Silva, the Neapolitan consul at Leghorn. But in May 1790 the British Foreign Secretary, the Duke of Leeds, instructed British representatives in Northern Italy to establish relations with "Paolo Rossi," with the aim of bringing him to London. This initiative derived from a meeting held between Francisco de Miranda and William Pitt, the prime minister, in which the Venezuelan had suggested the desirability of recruiting a few former Jesuits from Spanish America, both for their advice and in order to influence public opinion in their respective countries. If Pitt was prepared to listen to Miranda's proposals, it was because in 1790 Spain and Great Britain almost came to war over the latter's claims to settle Nootka Sound, near Vancouver, a move which the Spaniards resisted. To implement the scheme, the Under-Secretary of State at the Foreign Office, James Bland Burges, despatched his personal agent, a Mr. Sundersberg, to Italy. After meeting the Peruvian, Sundersberg reported that Viscardo "is a very strange and mistrustful man, albeit sincere and honest and appears to be very spoilt and careful of himself; he is well thought of and occupies an advantageous position and is of good life…." It was this favourable situation that allowed Viscardo to negotiate good terms of employment, since the British government agreed to pay him £200 a year and another £200 a year until his properties in Peru were restored to him. This salary allowed the Jesuit to live comfortably in London, since the official salary of Bland Burges as Under-Secretary was only £1,500, albeit supplemented in his case by private means.[13]

It was in March 1791 that Viscardo arrived in London, destined to remain there until his death in February 1798. He soon met and corresponded with Bland Burges, whom he later referred to as "my protector."[14] But these were uneasy years in Europe, when its monarchs all viewed with astonishment and apprehension the dramatic events in France that followed the convocation of the Estates General in 1789. It was also a time when poets and philosophers hailed the advent of a new age, since promulgation of the Declaration of the Rights of Man and the Citizen was widely interpreted as marking a watershed in the political history of Europe. In England, however, Pitt's government watched with growing concern as the Revolution pitched ever deeper into Jacobinism, and in 1793 Britain joined the Continental Coalition against the democratic regime in Paris. It was thus an unpropitious moment for Viscardo to present projects for the liberation of Spanish America since Britain had not merely settled its dispute with Spain over the Nootka Sound, but in 1793 became its ally in the war against France.

In the years 1791–92, following his arrival in London, Viscardo revised and completed no less than four separate papers, which drew on his previous research and on information provided by fellow Jesuits.[15] These were entitled:

1. *Projet pour rendre l'Amérique Espagnole indépendante. Suite du précédent projet.* (Project to achieve the independence of Spanish America together with the continuation of this project).

2. *Essai historique des troubles de l'Amérique Méridionale dans l'an 1780.* (Historical essay on the troubles of South America in the year 1780).

3. *Esquisse politique sur l'état actuel de l'Amérique Espagnole, et sur les moyens d'adresse pour faciliter son indépendance.* (Political sketch of the present state of Spanish America and on the means of address to hasten its Independence).

4. *Lettre aux Espagnols-Américains.* (Letter to the American Spaniards).

These manuscripts were supplemented by letters written both at the time and up to the year 1795. By then Viscardo had already begun a longer work which was to remain uncompleted, albeit in several drafts, at his death. The title of this work was:

5. *La Paix et le bonheur du siècle prochain. Remonstrance adressée à tous les peuples libres ou qui veulent l'etre. Par un américain espagnol.* (The Peace and happiness of the next century. Remonstrance to all free peoples or those who wish to be. By a Spanish American).

III

In his "Project to achieve the independence of Spanish America," written at Leghorn in 1790 but continued in London, Viscardo urged the British government to seek "the glory and utility" of liberating the New World from the Spanish yoke. He estimated that it would not require a force superior to that employed by Admiral Anson in his attack on Cartagena in 1742. However, he warned Bland Burges that it was essential to avoid any appearance of a conquest. The first step, therefore, was for Parliament to debate the matter and then to issue a public declaration of the independence of the Spanish American colonies. Such a declaration would stir the imagination of the creoles and induce them to accept the presence of the British. Indeed, such weight did Viscardo give to the role of imagination that he suggested that a prince of the royal family should head the expedition, since his very presence "would excite spirits and have more effect than the greatest force." So taken was Viscardo with this idea that he added: "Only Princes can truly undertake the heroic role of Liberators in the midst of so many objects of seduction...." After all, "the enthusiasm of having a king among a people who have no ideas other than of monarchy" would at once legitimize the cause of independence and attract both the ambitious and the timorous, not to mention those enamoured of novelty.

At the conclusion of his "Political Sketch," Viscardo returned to the necessity of capturing the imagination of the creoles by the simultaneous display of great force and the proclamation of independence. Since the American Spaniards had no desire to become the subjects of a foreign power, it would be necessary to circulate a manifesto justifying the break with Spain. Finally, in a letter of March 1793 he once more suggested that members of the British royal family might well be invited to accept thrones in America, since "the Spaniards of the New World appear, in all circumstances, to be incapable of republican ideas...."[16]

In the "Project" for independence, Viscardo suggested that a British naval expedition carrying some 6,000 soldiers might take the port of Arantac, situated only eighteen leagues from Arequipa, where his family was known and he himself had friends. From there it was only another eighty leagues to Cuzco. Another possibility might be to seize Maracaibo and from there either march to Caracas or Cartagena, in the latter case climbing through the mountains to Tunja, the scene of the 1780 revolt. But in the continuation of his project, written in England, he now pitched upon Coquimbo, a port in northern Chile which possessed a sheltered bay, was surrounded by a fertile countryside, was well supplied with both wheat and livestock, and had a good source of water. Here would be an ideal place for the squadron to recover from any damage incurred in the passage round Cape Horn, especially since it was distant from Santiago and over 150 leagues from Peru. It would thus constitute a base from which a strong fleet could blockade Lima and disrupt both inter-regional trade and the collection of customs revenue. Once its presence was felt it would be relatively easy to liberate Chile and then land a force at Pisco with the aim of reaching Arequipa.

In his subsequent "Political Sketch," Viscardo revised his project once more and now recommended that a strong squadron should be sent to the port of Concepción. Once there, the admiral in command should issue a declaration of Chilean independence under British protection, albeit allowing the inhabitants to choose the form of government which best suited their interests. He should then invite the Spanish Americans to form a deputation and approach the bishop, taking good care not to antagonize the clergy. Pursuing his fancy, Viscardo envisaged the population being attracted by martial music and cavalry exercises, not to mention the sale of English merchandise. At the appropriate moment, the local militia should be mobilized and Spanish government be brought to an end. If the European Spaniards in the city resisted these manœuvres they were to be offered repatriation to the Peninsula, or else dealt with in appropriate fashion. By way of compensation to Great Britain for the expenses incurred in this venture, he offered the island of Puerto Rico, since by then he no doubt had realized that British possession of Buenos Aires might well create problems in South America.[17]

In his accompanying "Historical Essay," written in 1792, Viscardo asserted that by reason of its Revolution, "under the mask of moderation and humanity, France aspires to convert itself into the first engine of humankind and the convergent point of all its interests through the attraction of universal Liberty." If France was to break off relations with Spain, it would move at once to proclaim the independence of the Spanish colonies and thereby deprive England of all the glory and profit that would accrue from achieving their emancipation. In the same way that the Anglo-Americans acknowledged their debt to France, so equally the Spanish Americans would honour France for its assistance. What was already clear was that "the Revolution in France is going to disturb all humankind" and that the American Spaniards were already cognizant of its principles. So great was Viscardo's detestation of the French revolutionary state that, in 1793, he forwarded to Bland Burges a letter from an Italian correspondent in which the French invaders were harshly denounced for their crimes and dismissed as villainous tigers.[18]

But Viscardo's hopes of British intervention were dashed to the ground when, in March 1793, France declared war on Spain, thereby causing Charles IV to ally his country with Britain. On 14 March of that year Viscardo wrote to Bland Burges to confess his dismay and cited commercial and fiscal statistics which indicated that Spanish trade with its colonies had grown greatly during recent years and that the accompanying increase in revenue had allowed ministers to build a powerful navy. The interests of Britain and Spain in the New World were always at odds, and if Britain took advantage of French maritime weakness to occupy Saint Domingue and other French colonies in the Caribbean, Spanish mistrust was bound to increase. At this point in his argument, Viscardo quoted his favourite maxim from Montesquieu's *Spirit of the Laws* (1748):

> The Indies and Spain are two powers under the same master; but the Indies are the principal, while Spain is only the accessory. It is vain for politics to attempt to bring back the principal to the accessory; the Indies will always draw Spain to themselves.

Once the effect of the two great revolutions in France and the Thirteen Colonies was fully assimilated, there was bound to be a great effervescence in the Spanish colonies, especially if they saw the French islands liberated. In effect, Spain had approached a watershed: either it could regain the affection of its colonists and become a great power, or it would be confronted with a sudden revolution in America. For his part, Viscardo doubted whether peace could continue but was persuaded that its continuance could only benefit Spain. As regards British interests, he observed that without its empire Spain's power would collapse and henceforth be of no concern. By contrast, with independence, the Spanish colonies would prosper and offer a bounteous market for British merchandise. For all that, it would be wise for the government to ascertain all it could as regards the basic facts and figures of Spanish trade, industry, and taxation. His own knowledge, Viscardo added, was out of date, since he had left Peru twenty-five years ago. In consequence he suggested that with the new treaty of alliance he should be sent to Cadiz under a false passport, so that he could gather information and take soundings as to the current sentiments of his compatriots.[19]

Although it is doubtful that Viscardo went to Spain, no further correspondence with Bland Burges has been found until February 1795, when in timid fashion he once more presented a project for liberating Spanish America. By that year, it had become clear that Great Britain had emerged from the conflict with France as the great commercial and maritime power. What Viscardo now suggested was that the United States should be brought into play and that, through an alliance with Britain, the emancipation of Spanish America be realized. By this stage he no longer sought to project any expeditions. It was with considerable delight that in August of that year he welcomed the news that Spain had been forced into an ignominious peace treaty with France, since he interpreted the event as accelerating the catastrophe that approached. Somewhat earlier, in June 1795, he had provided Bland Burges with a remedy for yellow fever prescribed in 1754 by Dr José de Gastelbonde, a "mulato doctor of the city of Cartagena," which had been reprinted in the *Gaceta de Madrid* in 1789.[20] If the Under-Secretary was interested in this matter, it was because British troops, who had been sent to occupy Saint Domingue, lay dying in their thousands, victims of a virulent outbreak of yellow fever.[21] With such advice, Viscardo justified his salary. With the retirement of his patron in October 1795, however, he wrote no further proposals for the liberation of his homeland and instead bent all his energies to framing his long dissertation on commerce, freedom, and peace.

Although Viscardo's monarchical projects might now appear fanciful, it should be noted that at much the same time Miranda still talked airily of establishing a hereditary "Inca" on a South American throne. More to the point, at the close of 1807 the British fleet escorted the Portuguese court across the Atlantic, thus allowing the Braganza dynasty to establish an empire in Brazil which lasted until 1889. So too, the liberator of Mexico, Agustín de Iturbide, established a short-lived empire in 1822. Where Viscardo might be criticized was in his pitching upon Great Britain as the power destined to effect the emancipation of Spanish America. For during the years 1793–98 British forces annexed, rather than liberated, a substantial part of Saint Domingue, restoring both slavery and plantation agriculture. In 1797 the island of Trinidad was occupied and its annexation recognized in the peace treaty of 1802. It was precisely during these years that Britain began the settlement of Australia; greatly extended its conquests in India; brutally suppressed the Irish rebellion of 1798; despatched its fleet to patrol the shipping lanes and coasts of the ocean seas; and in 1804 took possession of the Dutch colonies of the Cape of Good Hope and Ceylon.[22]

The achievement of Britain's naval hegemony was consummated at the battle of Trafalgar in 1805 when the combined fleets of France and Spain suffered outright defeat. Such was the imperial exuberance of these years that, in 1806–07, two successive British naval expeditions landed forces in Buenos Aires with the aim of converting that city and its hinterland into yet another colony. So effective was the resistance organized by local militia, however, that the invaders were obliged to stage a humiliating surrender and withdrawal. It was only after that defeat that the Secretary of State for War, Viscount Castlereagh, in a long memorandum dated 1 May 1807, concluded that any attempt to conquer such extensive countries as the River Plate, against the wishes of their inhabitants, was doomed to failure. The interest of Britain lay in opening the ports of Spanish America for trade and exploiting the commercial opportunities of the continent. It would be pleasing to imagine that, when Castlereagh reached this admirable conclusion, he had before him a copy of Viscardo's "Project"; but, since it was the custom in those days for officials to retain such memoranda for their own private collections, it is highly doubtful that any of Viscardo's papers were retained by the Foreign Office.[23] For all that, the British defeat at Buenos Aires indicated that Viscardo's analysis of the situation in Spanish America was accurate insofar as he had emphasized the necessity of a British expedition immediately issuing a proclamation of independence upon its arrival in port.

IV

In 1791–92 Viscardo wrote and presumably presented to the Foreign Office two essays, respectively entitled "Historical Essay" and "Political Sketch," in which he described the events of 1780–81 and analysed the current state of Spanish America. Despite occasional repetition, the two pieces can be discussed separately. To start with, although Viscardo claimed that the historical essay simply recapitulated from memory the substance of his letters to John Udney and Evan Nepean, in fact he now offered a revised, more accurate account of the Tupac Amaru rebellion. Indeed, his narrative follows closely, albeit in miniature, the description found in the unpublished *Dialogue* (1786), written by Melchor de Paz, the creole secretary of the viceroys Manuel de Guirior (1777–81) and Agustín de Jaúregui (1781–84).[24] He first noted that already in Cochabamba in 1730 and in Quito in 1764, the mestizos had rioted in furious protest against the insolent oppression of the European Spaniards. Only through the intervention of the creoles had the situation been brought under control. For all that, it was the Minister of the Indies, José de Gálvez (1776–87), who despatched Juan Antonio de Areche to Peru as visitor general, charged with the mission of raising taxes. At the same time, the infamous *repartimientos de comercio*, the enforced distribution of merchandise by corregidores, the district magistrates, reached a new level of abuse. The first signal of popular resistance was sounded in Arequipa, where the populace burnt the customs house to the ground and forced the European magistrates to flee the town. As elsewhere, it was the creoles who quietened the mob. But when José Gabriel Tupac Amaru, the cacique of Tinta, seized Antonio Arriaga, the local corregidor, and executed him for his oppression, he launched a rebellion that engulfed the entire highland area. All the leading cities were besieged; several massacres of creoles occurred; and Spanish rule was threatened.[25]

If the rebellion was suppressed, it was largely thanks to the leadership of two creole soldiers, Ignacio Flores, the new president of the high court at Charcas, and Manuel Villalta, a Limeño, who defended Cuzco with great skill and courage, and thereafter defeated the rebel forces in open battle. In describing the scene of Tupac Amaru's execution in the main square at Cuzco, Viscardo echoed Paz's *Dialogue* in recounting that when the visitor general, Areche, demanded that the rebel chieftain give the names of his accomplices, Tupac Amaru replied: "I only know of two…and these are you and I; you as the oppressor of my country and I because I have wished to rescue it from your tyrannies."[26] Although Viscardo refrained from citing the bishop of Cuzco's efforts to defend the city, he emphasized that Moscoso and many other priests, all accused of supporting the revolt, were exiled to Spain. Had it not been for the massacres, many creoles would have submitted to "a chief of this Nation," which is to say, to an Indian nobleman, since they were so hostile to colonial rule. At this point, Viscardo praised the superior leadership and policy of the uprising in New Granada, where the rebels obliged the archbishop to sign the Capitulations of Zipaquirá, under which the new taxes were withdrawn, the visitor general sent back to Spain, and creoles appointed as corregidores. This uprising at Socorro had denounced the *chapetones,* the European Spaniards, as foreigners and had formed "a plan of government almost completely republican," with only nominal dependence on Spain. What Viscardo failed to render explicit was that the movement in New Granada was ultimately controlled by the local creole elite.[27]

In his "Political Sketch," Viscardo sought to destroy the scornful image of Spanish America and its inhabitants presented in the celebrated histories of Guillaume Raynal and William Robertson, and in the travels of Antonio de Ulloa.[28] To this end, he compiled as much information as he could muster, obtaining data from several former Jesuits, most notably from Francisco Javier Clavijero, author of the widely acclaimed *Storia antica del Messico* (1780–81), and from Juan Ignacio Molina, author of a much translated geographical, natural, and civil history of Chile.[29] But whereas these scholars wrote learned accounts of their respective countries, and were at pains to defend the quality of the climate of the Americas, the rational abilities of the Indians, and the grandeur of ancient native civilisation, by contrast Viscardo participated in this grand debate over the New World in order to defend the talents of his creole compatriots and their claims for self government. At the same time, he aimed to provide his British patrons with an exact account of the current state of the Spanish colonies "in respect to their population, the character of their inhabitants and the organisation of a social system that results from the long conjunction of so many opposing and differing interests." Despite his early years in Cuzco, he exhibited no interest in the history of the Incas or in the greatness of their monuments. But the polemical purpose of his sketch was expressed at the outset when he observed: "With what aplomb should I, an unknown man, dare to contradict the most decided affirmations of Raynal, Robertson and Ulloa…?"[30]

As regards population, Viscardo drew upon estimates supplied by Clavijero, according to which the inhabitants of New Spain and central America governed by the three high courts of Guatemala, Mexico, and Guadalajara, numbered about eight million, of whom roughly a third were American Spaniards, mestizos, and mulattos. He then cited Ulloa's *Viaje a la América meridional* (1748), where the population of Quito was reckoned to be 552,800. Of more interest to the Foreign Office, no doubt, was the contrast he drew between the British and French islands in the Caribbean, where slaves formed the bulk of the population and hence were prone to revolt, and the situation on Cuba where, in 1778, out of a population numbering 171,828, only 48,929 were slaves. The conclusion he drew was that the Spanish islands were less exposed to rebellion, since the slaves were better treated, and could be more easily pacified. In all, he calculated that the total population of Spanish America was about 14 million, of whom some 5 million were creoles, mestizos, and mulattos. He was also at pains to list twenty-six cities, the combined total inhabitants of which numbered over a million, an estimate that might have been increased had he possessed better information about the urban population of New Spain.[31]

But it was the assertion of the philosophic historians of America that the absence of industry in the Spanish colonies left its inhabitants languishing in an impoverished rural hebetude which most offended Viscardo. He observed that the general conclusions of these authors did not square with their particular descriptions. Thus, for example, Ulloa gave an account of a thriving textile industry in the province of Quito, with cloth exported both to Chile and New Granada. Much the same could be said of Cuzco. So too, the city of Puebla in New Spain was renowned both for the quality of its cloth and of its ceramics. How, then, could the colonies be described as vegetating in indolence? Moreover, economic logic contradicted these generalizations, since the high prices of European imports caused by Spain's monopoly over colonial trade meant that at least three-quarters of the population had to dress themselves in local cloth. "Necessity has forced the barriers."[32]

Whereas Clavijero defended the rationality of the American Indians, Viscardo defended the character of the American Spaniards. Observing that Robertson and Raynal had both drawn on the writings of Ulloa when they framed such a scornful description of creole society, he complained that the Spanish traveller was clearly prejudiced, since "philosophy never made him forget that he was a *chapetón*." For favourable testimony, he cited the accounts written by two Italian Jesuits, Coleti and Gilij, who had praised the energetic, honourable, and generous character of the Spanish Americans. Indeed, even Ulloa had commented on the hospitable, loyal qualities of the Limeño nobility. These considerations were all the more important because the creoles exercised a decisive influence over all other classes and races, since they were "the soul and first engine of the Spanish colonies, for the same reasons as are the nobility, the bourgeoisie and clergy in all the states of Europe."[33] In effect, Viscardo defined his compatriots as the dominant social stratum in Spanish America, a colonial nobility denied its birthright, the governance of its own land.

Contrary to most pronouncements about the condition of the Indians, Viscardo adopted a positive view:

> In all that concerns the means of subsistence of individuals and in the regular operation of administration, the same excellent system established by the Incas has been maintained. Every village, every town of the Indians, has its own inalienable territory, in which a part belongs to the community for public necessities and the other part is distributed to each family for its sustenance and is generally found near each house.

So too, every village had its own cacique and their dignity and jurisdiction were respected by the Spaniards. The more wealthy caciques lived in comfort; they were treated as equals by the Spaniards; and their sons were at times educated in colleges in Lima, Cuzco, and Chuquisaca. Viscardo added that in all the public processions and solemnities in Cuzco, members of the Inca nobility sallied forth on the streets, dressed in their ancestral garments and carrying the royal standards. He commented: "I cannot but admire the profundity of a policy which has been applied, since it taught the Spaniards to respect the Indian nobility and persuaded the descendants of the Incas that they were truly honoured by these public distinctions." More generally, he concluded that although the Indians were greatly oppressed by the corregidores and their enforced distribution of merchandise, nevertheless, taken in the round, they were probably better off than the peasantry in such countries as Germany, Poland, and Russia.[34]

Turning to the social relations of the diverse races that inhabited Peru, Viscardo first observed that armed conquest, be it in Europe or America, was always accompanied by "iron, fire and desolation." Nevertheless, despite the system of feudalism which had separated conquerors from the conquered, in Europe the two sides had slowly come to form undivided nations. So also, in America once the violence of the conquest was ended, many of the heirs of the conquerors had Indian mothers, as Garcilaso de la Vega had testified. Moreover, the mestizos now comprised almost half the population and "this numerous race, as valiant as it is robust and intelligent, placed between the whites and the Indians, is the strongest link in the chain which unites these two classes in the same solid mass of society." In the highlands at least, most creoles had been suckled by Indian nurses to whom they were forever bound by natural affection. Their households retained Indian servants who were known for their loyalty. As parish priests, many creoles revived the spirit of Las Casas when they defended the Indians from the tyranny of the corregidores. In all this the whites were linked to the Indians by the operation "of natural cordiality for men with whom they had grown up together since infancy, whose language they spoke and whose customs they knew to the extent of adopting some of them." The real cause of social disorder, therefore, was the European Spaniards, who formed "a general league for mutual aid and support in whatever circumstance…" and nowhere more so than in commerce which they sought to monopolize. So divisive was the presence of European friars that in two of the provinces of the mendicant Orders their entry was prohibited. Yet although the creoles hated the *chapetones* who came to America, they remained loyal to the king of Spain, a loyalty that was in part religious in character. However, Viscardo commented that the court in Madrid "regards the creoles with mistrust," since America was treasured by all European Spaniards as "their common patrimony," the source of their greatness.[35]

In an illuminating excursus on recent history, Viscardo averred that at the close of the seventeenth century and during the reigns of Philip V and Ferdinand VI, numerous creoles had been appointed to high office, especially in the Church. Indeed, when he left Peru in 1768, out of its eight dioceses only the archbishopric of Lima was occupied by a European. So too, half the judges in the high court were creoles, even if these American lawyers had had to pay heavily for their places. It was José de Gálvez, the Minister of the Indies under Charles III, an inhuman monster with "a general and open hatred of the creoles," who had abrogated this policy and filled the courts and cathedrals with European Spaniards. So infuriated was this minister by the rebellions against the Crown that he had wanted to disarm all creoles, only then to fall prey to sudden death, caused possibly, so Viscardo surmised, by poison. Gálvez had been succeeded as minister by Antonio Porlier, "of much intelligence and practical knowledge of Peru," who at once sought to reconcile the creoles to Spanish rule. He had appointed the exiled bishop of Cuzco, Juan Manuel Moscoso, to be archbishop of Granada, and in New Spain had appointed as viceroy the Count of Revillagigedo, who had been born in America. So successful had been his policy that he had re-awakened "the affection" American Spaniards had for their king.[36]

If Viscardo blamed Gálvez both for provoking through Areche the Tupac Amaru revolt and for his alienation of the creole elite, he implicitly recognized the success of that minister's commercial policy when he signalized the great increase in trade between America and Spain which had occurred in recent years. Whereas in the epoch of the conquest, the New World had been mainly inhabited by semi-savage tribes, with only Peru and Mexico possessing advanced societies, by contrast there now existed a great continental empire, bound together by a common language and religion, linked by inter-regional trade and a growing prosperity. "The revolution in the policy of Spain as regards its relations with its colonies has been realized and there is now no way of retreat." The silver mines of New Spain and Peru had been revived to the point where total mintage of silver and gold from the entire empire now amounted to forty million pesos. Provinces such as Venezuela and Chile, which once had been mere frontier settlements, had experienced rapid growth in recent years. Indeed, Viscardo stated that the change in the last twenty years had been as great as that which had occurred in the last century in Russia. Even if Spanish rule continued, he predicted "a gradual increase in well-being" in Spanish America. All these considerations, however, led him once more to cite Montesquieu's famous dictum and to conclude that without the New World, Spain would be annihilated as a political power.[37]

In these essays Viscardo revealed the intensity of his creole patriotism and acted as the spokesman of the provincial nobility from which he sprang. He joined with fellow Jesuits in combating the prejudice and errors of the enlightened historians of America, defending the good name and character of his compatriots. His vision of colonial society was of a harmonious hierarchy of race and class which was disturbed only by the exploitation promoted by Spain and by the rapacity of the European Spaniards sent to govern America. Once the authority of the Spanish king was destroyed, then the creole nobility, lawyers, and clergy would assume their birthright, the governance of their country, albeit conceding an honourable role for the Indian nobility. In his account of the Bourbon reforms, Viscardo fixed upon Gálvez as the chief author of the measures that had provoked so much uproar and indeed testified that, until his accession as minister, creoles had enjoyed access to high office in Church and State. At the same time, he fixed upon the paradox that the reign of Charles III (1759–88) had witnessed an unprecedented growth in colonial trade and industry, an increase which had diffused a general prosperity throughout Spanish America. The very success of this economic policy had created circumstances which would eventually lead to independence.

v

In a letter addressed to Bland Burges dated 15 September 1791, Viscardo announced that he enclosed his *Letter Addressed to the American Spaniards,* in which he exhorted his compatriots to rebel against the colonial regime that oppressed them. Unlike his other compositions of these years, the *Letter* was written as a public manifesto, designed to be distributed by British naval expeditions if and when they landed in Spanish America. As such, it was distinguished by a passionate, rhetorical intensity. In his accompanying statement, Viscardo admitted that the *Letter* might well cause an insurrection and thus should only be distributed in case of war between Britain and Spain. But if hostilities were not opened, then Great Britain should employ all its influence to open Spanish American ports to international shipping. Moreover, British and Spanish engineers might be induced to collaborate on the survey and construction of a canal in Panama or Nicaragua to connect the oceans. In the long run, however, "the interests of all the human species demand that the sequestration of America should be lifted," since Spain could no longer be allowed to annul "the natural rights" of the inhabitants of the New World.[38]

28

The *Letter Addressed to the American Spaniards* opened with the declaration that the imminent advent of a new century marked the moment when it was necessary to proclaim that "The New World is our *patria* and its history is our history." But although the discovery of America was the greatest event in human history, for three centuries the Spanish colonies had suffered "ingratitude, injustice, serfdom and desolation." "Our fathers" had conquered this vast territory through their own expense and enterprise, sallying far beyond the sphere of royal domination, only to find that the Court of Spain failed to comply with the "agreements" and the "solemnly stipulated conditions" under which both Columbus and the conquerors had seized possession of America. Yet "our fathers" had remained loyal to their first *patria*, Spain, and had thus sacrificed the interests of their true *patria*, the New World, with the result that their descendants, the American Spaniards, were "slandered, persecuted and ruined." Taking advantage of their loyalty, the kings of Spain had promulgated laws and installed a colonial regime which actively harmed the prosperity and well-being of the inhabitants of their "immense empire" in America. They had treated the creoles not as heirs of the conquerors but as so many prisoners found guilty of unspecified crimes. If this were indeed the case, then what was Spanish government in the New World but "a cruel and open tyranny"? Had Viscardo so desired, he could have cited any number of classical texts beginning with Aristotle and Aquinas in which the tyrant was defined as the ruler who governed for his own profit rather than in the interests of his people.[39]

To substantiate his charge, however, Viscardo cited Spain's commercial monopoly and the excessive taxes it levied on trade with America. The effect of this "mercantile tyranny" was that the American Spaniards paid exorbitant prices for all imported goods and received low prices for their exported produce. Had not Antonio de Ulloa testified that in Quito imported iron cost twenty times its value in Europe? So too, despite the fertility of American vineyards, wine was often in short supply, even for holy mass, and was invariably expensive. All this was as nothing, however, compared to the violent oppression which accompanied the *repartimientos de comercio,* the enforced distribution, as noted earlier, of merchandise to Indians and mestizos by the corregidores, the predominantly European district magistrates. For three centuries "a horde of adventurers" had been despatched by the crown to govern the colonial empire, men simply intent on self enrichment, ruling without compassion or justice, "ceaselessly re-enacting those scenes of horror which wiped off the face of the earth whole peoples whose only crime was their weakness, so that these adventurers have converted the splendour of the greatest of conquests into the most ignominious dishonour for the name of Spain." Moreover, the Spanish Americans had not merely been deprived of any participation in the government of their own lands, they had witnessed the crown offering high office to foreigners of all nations, "considering us unworthy and unfit to hold those places which by the most rigorous right belong exclusively to us in our own *patria.*" The glory won by our forefathers had become a heritage of ignominy and the treasures of America have reduced us into a state of "misery and slavery."[40]

In this passionate indictment of Spanish rule, Viscardo drew upon a long tradition of creole patriotic protest against the misrule of European magistrates and the exploitation of European merchants. In the early seventeenth century, the Peruvian Franciscan Fr. Buenaventura de Salinas y Córdova

(1592–1653), the grandson of a conqueror, lamented that the sheer distance of Peru from Madrid had denied creoles easy access to the royal court, the fount of all favours and offices, so that the sons of the conquerors "through misfortune have lost their rights and privileges of descent." As it was, "newcomers and foreigners" were appointed as district magistrates. Moreover, immigrants from Spain also dominated commerce and were more to be feared by the creoles than the Dutch or English pirates, since not merely did they exploit the unfortunate Indians, they also sought to monopolize all honours and credit within the country. The source of most immigrant wealth usually lay in the ill-treatment of the natives, since these newcomers or upstarts "live among us squeezing the land like a sponge, sucking the blood of the Indians like mosquitoes." Although the creoles were equal to the European Spaniards in character and intelligence, they failed to obtain high office in Church and State owing to the crown's neglect and suffered the mortification of witnessing European magistrates enrich themselves through systematic injustice.[41] In thus re-stating these time-honoured grievances of the American Spaniards, Viscardo almost instinctively sought to arouse the deeply ingrained creole mistrust of peninsular Spaniards and the creole resentment of their colonial condition.

Where Viscardo advanced beyond the traditional plaints of creole patriotism was in his condemnation of the absolute monarchy established by the Habsburgs and later reinforced by the Bourbons. In the Middle Ages, following the ruin of the Gothic empire, "our ancestors" concentrated all judicial, fiscal, and legislative power "in the Cortes which represented the Nation in its different classes" and acted as the guardian of "the rights of the people." In his commentaries on the laws of Aragon, Jerónimo Blanca had celebrated "the Justiciar," a magistrate charged with the maintenance of the laws and liberties of the kingdom, even when confronted with royal power. At their coronation, the kings of Aragon had solemnly sworn to observe the laws and were reminded that if they disregarded them they would cease to be sovereigns. It was this noble spirit of liberty, so Viscardo averred, that had endowed "our ancestors" with the enterprise and vigour that had enabled them to encompass a hemisphere within a generation. When Charles V sought to govern through his Flemish favourites, the Spaniards had rebelled. But they had failed to prevent the crown from establishing its absolute authority, that "supreme economic power," as it was now styled, which allowed the king to govern in an arbitrary fashion without rendering account to his subjects. Examination of "our national history" thus revealed how great had been the revolution in "the constitution and government of Spain." In this attack on royal absolutism, Viscardo anticipated Spanish jurists and statesmen such as Francisco Martínez Marina and Gaspar Melchor de Jovellanos who, in the years 1806–10, lauded Spain's ancient constitution and sought to reform the monarchy by a return to medieval institutions and liberties.[42]

In Peru the first great exponent of the new-found arbitrary power of the Spanish monarchy was Viceroy Francisco de Toledo, who seized the last heir of the Inca empire, "the young, innocent Tupac Amaru" and submitted him to judicial murder. Moreover, Viscardo cited the Inca Garcilaso de la Vega on Toledo's pursuit and torture of the young mestizos of Cuzco, the offspring of Spanish conquerors and Inca princesses, whom he accused of supporting the rebel chieftain. Indeed, Viscardo directly cited the great mestizo historian when he described the fate of his compatriots:

Those…whose mothers were daughters or nieces of the Inca family, and whose fathers were Spaniards and of the first conquerors who acquired so much fame and reputation, nevertheless, were so little esteemed, that neither by reason of the natural right of their mothers nor by the merits and great services of their fathers, were they given anything.

To this bitter statement Viscardo added the lament of an Indian mother of a persecuted mestizo that she regretted ever giving birth to such an unfortunate son. As Garcilaso had noted, the new governors conferred all posts on their friends and relatives, so that the children of the conquerors were obliged to beg for their subsistence or were forced into robbery, often hanged thereafter for their offences. When Viscardo thus cited Garcilaso, he signalized the difference between the conquerors and the society they had established and the arbitrary colonial regime introduced by Philip II and Toledo. At the same time, he associated the cause of the Spanish Americans with the fate of the mestizos of Cuzco.[43]

For a contemporary demonstration of royal tyranny what more glaring example could be found than the expulsion of over 5,000 Jesuits from the territories of the monarchy? Here was a body of men, all Spanish citizens, renowned for their services to the community, who possessed great riches and enjoyed high public esteem. And yet without any reason ever being given, they were abruptly arrested and sent into a penurious exile. It would be hard to encounter "so insolent a violation of all the principles and fundamental laws of right and justice." No matter what the form of government, "the preservation of natural rights and especially of liberty and security of persons and of goods is unquestionably the fundamental basis of all human society." The arbitrary character of the expulsion destroyed the very expectation that the rights of individuals to liberty and property would be respected. If the crown had driven the Jesuits, both European and American, into exile, it was because it wanted to confiscate their wealthy properties. So too, the events of 1780 had been caused by the crown's collection of new taxes, impositions which had prompted such a noble resistance from the Spaniards of New Granada. And all this had been followed by the raising of militia forces in the Indies and the enlargement of the Spanish navy by means of revenue levied in the New World. What is most striking in this litany of abuse was Viscardo's omission of any discussion of the Tupac Amaru revolt, clear evidence of his addressing his letter to the American Spaniards, many of whom had fought to defeat that movement.[44]

   With so much evidence of tyranny across three centuries, the time had come, Viscardo declared, for the Spanish Americans to emulate the "great examples of our ancestors" and decide "to be a different people." After all, had not Montesquieu, that "great genius," written that "the Indies and Spain are two powers under the same master; but the Indies are the principal and Spain is but secondary." Like a bad schoolmaster, Spain had lived in opulence off the goods of its pupil. The Court had ignored "the inalienable rights of all men and the indispensable duties of all governments." In consequence there now approached "the moment which nature, reason and justice have signalized for our emancipation from such a tyrannical tutelage." Already both Holland and Portugal had broken away from Spain. So too, the English colonies had been the first "to crown the New World with an independent sovereignty." In a clear echo of Thomas Paine's *Common Sense* (1776), possibly refracted through its paraphrase in Raynal's *History* (1781), Viscardo declared that "nature has separated us from Spain by means of immense seas" and this alone proclaimed "our natural independence." Just as a son separated from his father by a great distance had the natural right to emancipate himself from parental authority, so equally the American Spaniards had the right to independence. What good could come from a government situated three or four thousand miles away and which sought at all times to benefit its own industry and trade? Viscardo concluded by the assertion of both ancestral and natural rights. The American Spaniards were obliged by the "sacred gratitude to our ancestors who did not prodigally spill their blood and sweat that the theatre of their glory and toil might be that of our slavery and misery." But, at the same time, they possessed "the natural rights we have received from our Creator," the rights of reason and liberty, which would form the most precious heritage of their descendants. It was a blasphemy against the Creator to imagine that he had created the New World for the enrichment of "a few imbecile rogues."[45]

With his case now presented, Viscardo called upon his compatriots to put an end forever to tyranny and inhumanity and to establish a "wise liberty." So just was their cause that even wise Spaniards, who still groaned under oppression in their *patria*, would applaud "our noble enterprise in causing the re-birth of the national glory" and many, no doubt, would seek asylum and be welcomed with fraternal hospitality. The next century would thus witness men of all nations frequenting the shores of America, attracted by the free exchange of their products; indeed, with despotism and poverty banished, such men would settle in Spanish America, coming "to enrich us with their industry, their knowledge, and especially by the increase of our population." In this way, America would be joined together with the most distant parts of the earth and its inhabitants would form "a single great family of brothers." In this conclusion Viscardo attested to the cosmic euphoria which haunted the imagination of Europe during the first stages of the French Revolution. In any case, had not Thomas Paine already declared that "the cause of America is in great measure the cause of all mankind"?[46]

When Viscardo sent the French translation of his *Letter* to the Foreign Office, he clearly presented it as a manifesto that was written for immediate publication in London and distribution in Spanish America by a British naval expedition. It was thus designed to inflame public opinion and pre-dispose creoles to rebellion. What rendered the *Letter* so effective was precisely its combination of traditional creole plaints with the Enlightenment's insistence on natural rights. In his citation of "inalienable rights" to liberty, security, and property, Viscardo echoed both the Declaration of Independence of 1776 and the Declaration of the Rights of Man of 1789. But whereas Thomas Jefferson only offered a list of the tyrannies of George III as grounds of a separation from Britain, by contrast, Viscardo began his case with Toledo's execution of Tupac Amaru and characterized all three centuries of colonial rule as despotic. The emphasis on contemporary political issues was thus in part replaced by an historical indictment.

The peculiarity of Viscardo's combination of ancestral and natural rights can be defined by a comparison with the Abbé Sieyès' *What Is the Third Estate?* (1789). Sieyès had sharply criticized, as an intolerable expression of privilege, the French aristocracy's citation of the Frankish conquest as the foundation of their ancestral rights.[47] By contrast, Viscardo was at pains to reiterate that the creoles' right to govern America derived from its conquest by their forefathers. Moreover, whereas Sieyès identified the nation as the source of sovereignty and the rights of its citizens, Viscardo failed to devise any common nomenclature that might designate the diverse races of Peru, even if he did assert that they "almost formed a people." In effect, Viscardo belonged to a generation and a social milieu in which the term "Americans" had yet to be applied to describe all the inhabitants of the New World. Indeed, his text suggests that he still conceived of the creoles as members of the Spanish nation, albeit natives of an American rather than a European *patria*. When he addressed his *Letter* to the American Spaniards, he thus had in mind the Peruvian equivalents of the European "nobility, bourgeoisie and clergy." His manifesto expressed the interests and sentiments of a colonial nobility which had been denied its birthright, the governance of the country conquered and settled by its ancestors. But this traditional plaint was matched by an equally vehement insistence on universal natural rights and topped by a Utopian expectation that Spanish America was destined to become the resort of all humanity. It was precisely this unstable compound that rendered the *Letter* such a potent political instrument, since it spoke in different voices to different readers.

The impact of the *Letter* upon the men who promoted and fought for the independence of Spanish America is difficult to estimate with any precision. The Venezuelan Pedro Gual testified that he had read Viscardo's work with "holy enthusiasm," a phrase that Miranda also adopted.[48] So impressed was Mariano Moreno, the first secretary of the Argentine Junta of 1810, that when still a lawyer in

Chuquisaca he made his own Spanish translation of the French edition of the *Letter*.[49] The degree to which Fray Servando Teresa de Mier, the Mexican ideologue, took his arguments directly from Viscardo is not clear. An ardent creole patriot, Mier drew on much the same tradition as Viscardo, read many of the same contemporary authors, and emphasized the ancestral rights of his compatriots. Yet we know that the former Dominican possessed a copy of Viscardo's letter. But Mier developed these traditional arguments into a form of proto-nationalism when, in rejecting the idea that Spain was the mother country of Mexico, he affirmed that many conquerors and later settlers had bred with Indian women, so that "we creoles are all mestizos.... In our veins flows the pure blood of the native lords of this country." In a memorial published in Philadelphia in 1821, Mier complained of recent Spanish territorial treaties with the United States and added:

> All these concessions are insults we suffer, not only on account of the rights of our mothers who were Indians, but also by reason of the pacts of our fathers, the conquerors, who gained everything at their own cost and risk, with the kings of Spain. America is ours because our fathers gained it, thus creating a right; because it was of our mothers; and because we are born in it. This is the natural right of all peoples in their respective regions. God has separated us from Europe by an immense sea and our interests are distinct. Spain never had any right here.[50]

In this passage we surely observe the influence of Viscardo's *Letter,* and nowhere more so than in the idiosyncratic combination of the Inca Garcilaso de la Vega and Tom Paine.

In a letter to Bland Burges dated 6 August 1795, Viscardo boldly announced that "I have now dedicated myself to an important project, intended to demonstrate that Europe is unlikely to obtain the lasting and firm peace it so much needs before establishing a general freedom of trade, which by its very nature will be converted into a bond uniting all peoples." In effect, he had failed thus far to complete the dissertation on colonial commerce which he had mentioned as early as 1791. And, though he sent one last letter to his patron in the Foreign Office in which he set down any number of statistics dealing with the mintage of silver coin in Spanish America and the Atlantic trade, he did not succeed in finishing an extended draft of his treatise until 1797. But Bland Burges retired from office in October 1795 and there is little to suggest that the final version of Viscardo's dissertation was written for perusal by the British government.[51] For it was entitled, "The Peace and happiness of the next century," and was described as "an exhortation addressed to all free peoples or those who wish to be free, by a Spanish American." Although it presented a wide range of economic statistics and arguments, it also contained a great deal of enlightened humanitarianism. Of creole patriotism there is but a trace. The treatise thus signalized a marked change or development in Viscardo's thinking and identified him as a disciple, no matter how partial or idiosyncratic, of the European Enlightenment.

No element of Viscardo's dissertation is more surprising than its exordium, which offered a ringing condemnation of war as "the most cruel scourge that has ever afflicted humanity." What was the current conflict but a continuation of the wars that devastated Europe for the last fifty-seven years, which was to say, since the outbreak of the war of the Austrian Succession? If an enduring peace was not reached, then "the ambition of a murderous glory" would yield a more grievous harvest of death. Had not Montesquieu long since commented on the growth in the size of armies and the increase in taxes needed to support them?[52] So also he cited Fénelon's *Télémaque* (1699) in which the Archbishop of Cambrai described the devastation caused by aggressive warfare and called for a League of Princes dedicated to peace.[53] And yet at the moment that Viscardo wrote, the peoples of Europe saw their continent "drenched with tears and blood, covered with corpses and ruins" and hungered desperately for peace. Surely the time had come when a government might announce new principles of political action, a time when "Humanity, justice, reason and universal morality would dictate a new code of the Law of Nations, cleansed forever from the filthy rust of the barbarous ages." In this exordium, Viscardo thus identified himself as a disciple of Fénelon and the Abbé Saint-Pierre, and as a devoted reader of the concluding book of Raynal's *History*.[54]

Although Viscardo's condemnation of war no doubt sprang from Christian aversion to the pursuit of vainglory so clearly expressed by Fénelon, it was justified by appeal to the contemporary doctrine, already advanced by Montesquieu, that "the natural effect of trade is to bring peace." Among "enlightened nations" it was already accepted that "at present the true measure of power is the prosperity of commerce, the father of industry…." More to the point, in his *Wealth of Nations* (1776) Adam Smith had argued that the fruits of trade were good government, liberty, individual security, and peace since, as much for nations as for individuals, commerce formed "a bond of union and friendship." The economic theorist added that in the future, war would be seen as more destructive of prosperity than profitable and that free trade would be accepted as the source of universal well-being. As is well known, Smith also condemned mercantilism and the monopoly over colonial commerce which it advocated.[55] Within these declarations, however, there was an implicit argument. In the *Spirit of the Laws*, Montesquieu had argued that whereas most monarchies engaged in warfare, by contrast, republics preferred peace and trade. So also, when Fénelon condemned warfare, he attributed its cause to the aggressive ambition of absolute monarchs. In effect, the unspoken premise of Viscardo's exordium, present in his sources, was a preference for republican forms of government. So also, it contained an implicit repudiation of the chief tenet of creole patriotism, the insistence on ancestral rights based on conquest.[56]

Entering into the substance of his treatise, Viscardo framed a critical portrait of colonial commerce and taxation, replete with statistical demonstrations drawn from a surprising range of sources. He cited "the inestimable work" of Jerónimo de Ustariz, *Theórica y práctica de comercio* (1756), Bernardo Ward, *Proyecto económico* (1779), "the most perfect work of its kind that has appeared in Spain"; and even reversed his opinion of Antonio de Ulloa, praising his "sagacity, wit and respect for the truth," albeit noting that his prejudice against both creoles and Indians was contradicted by his own testimony. But in addition to the standard histories of Robertson and Raynal, he also drew on travellers such as Jean-François Bourgoing's *Nouveau voyage en Espagne* (1789) and Joseph Townsend's *A Journey through Spain* (1792); read Pedro Rodríguez Campomanes' *Discurso sobre el fomento de la industria popular* (1774); and consulted both the *Gaceta de Madrid* and the *Mercurio Peruano*. In effect, the ex-Jesuit here emerged as a learned disciple of the Spanish Enlightenment, albeit concerned to demonstrate that without freedom, prosperity and even the power of the state were bound to decline, a lesson that the kings of Spain had neglected for three centuries. Both Spain and America were thus the victims of the same despotism. He lamented that, if at the beginning of the sixteenth century Spain was still a prosperous country endowed with a thriving commerce and a strong fleet, the subsequent discovery of Potosí had distorted the basis of the Spanish economy. Henceforth, it was characterized by monopoly and an insensate pursuit of gold and silver. In Peru the enforced recruitment of the Indian peasantry for labour in the mines had led to depopulation and devastation. Much the same was true of Mexico, where in the northern province of Sonora there was no industry and all the profits earned from mining were consumed in the purchase of European merchandise. And yet, as José de Acosta, the celebrated Jesuit chronicler, had observed, nature in America was so fertile and abundant in produce that the continent should have supported a lively exchange of provincial goods.[57]

The analytical core of Viscardo's case against Spanish colonialism was located in his analysis of the effects of the famous decree of *Comercio Libre* of 1778, which opened the chief ports of the Peninsula and America for trade by individual, licensed shipping. The superficial results had been impressive. Between 1753 and 1786 the value of exports from the New World to Spain had more than doubled. In that latter year the overall value had reached almost 52 million pesos, of which 36 million consisted of gold and silver and the remainder of colonial produce. These estimates could be confirmed by the reported production of the American mints, which revealed that the overall coinage of gold and silver had reached 38 million pesos.

If we compare these figures with those presented by Alexander von Humboldt in his *Political Essay on the Kingdom of New Spain* (1807–11), we find that they are in substantial agreement.[58] But Viscardo emphasized the heavy incidence of taxation on all goods, be they imports or exports, leading him to refer to "the fiscal hydra with its hundred frightful heads." More to the point, he analysed the composition of Spanish revenue and concluded that, if both tobacco monopoly profits and the customs duties charged at Spanish ports on imports from America were included, then the direct fiscal tribute from the New World accruing to the crown was 14.8 million pesos. It was thanks to American revenue that Spain had been able to rebuild its fleet and once more figure in the European concert as a maritime power. Despite these impressive achievements, Spain was not a phoenix reborn from its ashes, since as Montesquieu had observed, "the king of Spain ... is a very rich individual in a very poor state." Viscardo ridiculed the claims put about by government ministers that about half of all exports to America were produced in Spain, adding sarcastically, "the government is the only public novelist in all the Spanish monarchy." Had not Campomanes deplored the backwardness of Spanish industry? Moreover, Bourgoing had found that a good part of the manufactured goods sent abroad were in fact of French origin, but simply stamped as Spanish, so as to pay a lower rate of customs duty. Without liberty there was no chance that industry could ever thrive in the Peninsula, still less satisfy the demands of the American markets.[59]

In conclusion, Viscardo set down some elaborate calculations which demonstrated that the terms of trade between Peru and Spain were grossly unfair, since the costs of all imports were heavily inflated both by monopoly advantage and high taxation, whereas exports commanded low prices but were equally burdened by customs duties and, in the case of bullion, by any number of taxes levied by the crown. In this insistence on the unequal terms of trade as a defining feature of Spanish colonialism and as a significant cause of the economic backwardness of Spanish America, Viscardo anticipated the theses of Raul Prebisch and the Economic Commission for Latin America in the twentieth century.[60] But, whereas modern economists fixed upon the unequal exchange between the industrial metropolis and the primary producers of the periphery, the former Jesuit attributed the evil to colonial monopoly and taxation and presented free trade as the chief remedy for economic stagnation.

In accordance with his new-found revulsion from warfare, Viscardo framed a harsh indictment of the Spanish conquest. Citing Robertson, he noted that, on landing in Cuba, Columbus had been welcomed by the local king in a noble act of humanity, only then to subject the natives of that island to enslavement and eventual extermination. The depopulation of the Indies had been registered by Bartolomé de las Casas in his *Brevísima relación de la destrucción de las Indias* (1552), a work which could be compared to Banquo's ghost, a constant reminder to the Spanish government that its name was stained forever by the massacre of the natives of the New World. So too, Viscardo cited Benito Jerónimo Feijoo, who in his *Teatro crítico universal* (1726–39) had commented that during those years the Indians had seen the Spaniards as gods, whereas the Spaniards had treated the Indians worse than animals. Moreover, such was the conquerors' hunger for gold that it could be said that one form of idolatry was substituted for another, since where once the unfortunate natives were sacrificed to pagan idols, they were now sacrificed to the god of gold.[61] After the conquest, Viscardo added, the Indians lost all their natural rights and if they resisted were enslaved. He portrayed an imaginary council of Philip II sitting down like a gang of wolves about to feed off sheep, as they authorized the enslavement of the Indians. Nor did the situation of the natives improve over the years, since the bishop of Quito, Alonso de la Peña Montenegro (1652–88), had described them as "these weak and miserable beings," who were oppressed by excessive tribute and onerous labour services. Indeed, Viscardo commented: "The Indians of today are in the same state of misery as their grandfathers; and the author of this work has been witness of this since his infancy in Peru," an admission that ran contrary to his earlier affirmations of social harmony.[62]

Nor had the creoles benefited from their superior status, for although they maintained the empire in America, they were despised and mistrusted by the Court and by reason of royal despotism were condemned to live out their days suffering inertia, abjection, and oppression. Although liberty, property, and individual security were the primary objects of all government and society, they were denied these natural rights, so that "the Spanish New World is no more than an immense prison for its inhabitants; only the agents of despotism and monopoly were free to enter and leave." As Rousseau had argued in his *Social Contract* (1762), the primary test of good government was the increase in population.[63] Yet, whereas in the New World the Spanish colonies could have supported 150 million inhabitants, at present all they maintained was 13,220,000. By contrast, the population of the United States was doubling in every generation, as Benjamin Franklin had demonstrated, and already stood at over five million. What better proof of the effects of liberty could there be than this comparison? But then, as Montesquieu had argued, the British constitution was a model of freedom and had been applied to the British colonies. Pursuing another thesis of his French master, Viscardo described the oriental despotism of the Ottoman Turks, only to note that its taxes were low and that it permitted a free flow of trade with Europe, allowing its subjects to profit from this exchange. In his view the comparison did not favour Spain, whose empire could be defined as "the *Non plus ultra* in the matter of despotism." If only Spain had emulated ancient Greece and allowed its colonies self-government, then other Europeans would have come to form a new Europe in America, and Spain would have won an immortal name for itself.[64] As always, the point of such comparisons was to demonstrate the shortcomings of the colonial regime. In the eighteenth century the hispanic world already lived under the shadow of external comparison and in offering the United States as a model of liberty and prosperity, Viscardo acted as a precursor of what was to become a nineteenth-century commonplace.

Nothing revealed more clearly the effect of the Enlightenment on Viscardo than his critical comments on Roman and Spanish Catholicism. This is not a matter which admits any easy judgement. In his only letter which dealt directly with religion, written on 1 May 1787 to a fellow ex-Jesuit, he criticized the Tuscan bishops and theologians who supported the Jansenist theses of the Synod of Pistoia.[65] But in his treatise on "Peace and Happiness," he deplored the establishment in the sixteenth century of "the most boundless civil and religious despotism," asserting that by reason of this double despotism "the general prosperity, the glory and old great national character were eclipsed to the point of leaving no more trace than their memory." On describing the role of religion in the conquest of America, he first affirmed that "superstition" had perverted the "natural innocence of the primitive morality of men" and had then found expression in fanaticism, discord, and the sword. It had been "the chief of the Roman Church" acting as "master, king, great father and governor of all men," who had conferred temporal sovereignty over America on the kings of Spain. A religion which breathed universal benevolence had been employed as a cloak to justify the violation of the rights Nature had conceded to the Indians. In all this, the Courts of Rome and Spain had consulted only their ambitions and, acting in contempt of the rights of Nature, had reduced the New World to "political, civil and religious slavery."[66] In this context he cited Montesquieu, when he asked "how many victims has the Inquisition sacrificed to the demon of intolerance?" But it was not merely the political use of Catholicism to which Viscardo objected since, on lamenting the abuses committed by Spaniards, he also criticized Catholic devotions when he observed:

> Would that they remember that an eternal and just Providence watches over the moral order, the most important part of creation, and that masses, confessions and heavenly advocates cannot change this immutable order and still less those impious superstitions that have ideas about the Divinity that are more absurd and outrageous than those of Atheism.[67]

By the end of his life, Viscardo had obviously come to adopt a philosophical or enlightened version of Christianity that viewed with disdain both the pretensions of the Papacy and the devotional practices of contemporary Catholicism. It was an attitude also found among many so-called Jansenists of this epoch.

In conclusion, Viscardo asserted that by reason of their recognition of the independence of the United States, all free peoples had implicitly acknowledged the right of other colonies to achieve their independence. Here was a universal bond of humanity. In any case, since Spain had supported the liberation of the Thirteen Colonies, the Spanish people should actively seek to free their own colonies. Looking to the future, he saw in Spanish America a rich market for European industry. Whereas Asia, so he averred, was a poor trading partner, since it possessed many manufactures, by contrast Spanish America formed a perfect complement to Europe. With free trade and the cessation of high taxation would come peace, liberty, and a more plenteous exchange of agricultural produce for European manufactures. The effect of commerce was such that "far from exciting the spirit of mistrust and exclusion, it cannot but consolidate concord, through very avarice, no matter how blind the projects it pursues." The self-interest of economic man, engaged in reciprocal exchange, would thus inevitably yield beneficial results.[68] As in the *Letter*, Viscardo ended on a euphoric note, asserting that, thanks to independence and free trade, Spanish America would enter a virtuous cycle of peace and prosperity.

Although "The Peace and happiness of the next century" certainly indicated Viscardo's abandonment of creole patriotism and his espousal of the liberal tenets of the Enlightenment, it failed to provide any suggestion of how Spanish America was to govern itself after independence was achieved. If his condemnation of warfare as the scourge of humanity was matched by an implicit preference for republics animated by commercial values, he entirely eschewed any mention of the concept of the nation, which the French Revolution had elevated into the sole source and repository of political sovereignty. In part, of course, this omission can be explained by his premature death, since he never experienced the profound shock of the events of 1808–10, when French forces took possession of the Peninsula and thereby destroyed the traditional authority of the Spanish monarchy. It was only with the Constitution of Cadiz of 1812 that representative forms of government were introduced based upon the declaration that "sovereignty resides essentially in the nation," with the king reduced to the level of an hereditary executive. Obviously, at this point, the Spanish nation was still a concept, a legal fiction, especially since it was defined as comprising "all the Spaniards of both Hemispheres."[69] But merely to indicate these developments is to signalize the absence of the political dimension in Viscardo's thinking.

VII

In the early twentieth century, José de la Riva Agüero, a romantic nationalist, identified El Inca Garcilaso de la Vega as both precursor and prophet of modern Peru who, by reason of his parentage and writings, demonstrated that the historic nation derived its cultural being from both the Inca empire and the Spanish conquest.[70] In the late twentieth century, largely thanks to the discovery of his lost manuscripts, Juan Pablo Viscardo y Guzmán has come to occupy an analogous role in the Peruvian national tradition, where he figures both as precursor of independence and as prophetic witness of the crisis of creole patriotism at the close of the colonial era. There are haunting parallels and contrasts between the life and work of these two exiles. Garcilaso was a mestizo educated in Cuzco, who left Peru in 1560 at the age of twenty-one in order to live in Spain, where in provincial obscurity he slowly mastered the historiographical lessons of the Italian Renaissance. For his part, Viscardo was a highland gentleman with relatives among the Indian nobility, educated at Cuzco, who left Peru in 1768 at the age of twenty and, after a few years in Italy, moved to London, where he studied the economic doctrines of the European Enlightenment. Both these exiles were autodidacts. But whereas Garcilaso was welcomed by a Spanish uncle and established cordial relations with scholars in Córdoba, Viscardo, so it would appear, lived a solitary life in London, obliged to turn to a stranger, Rufus King, for reassurance and support. Garcilaso published his works of history and was buried with honour in the great mosque of Córdoba, by then converted into a Christian cathedral. Viscardo could only bequeath his manuscripts to posterity, and he lies in an unknown grave. For all that, both these men drew upon their boyhood memories to frame nostalgic idylls of a Peru which by the time they wrote had already disappeared. If Garcilaso excoriated Viceroy Toledo for his judicial murder of the young Tupac Amaru and his persecution of the mestizos, so also Viscardo condemned Areche's cruel execution of Tupac Amaru II and the exile of the Jesuits. In both cases, these Peruvian patriots shared a common enemy, the absolutist monarchy created by Philip II and fortified by Charles III, whose servants in the New World sought to extract the maximum profit from Spain's overseas empire.

If Viscardo has been defined as both a precursor of independence and as a prophetic witness to the crisis of creole identity, it was because his intellectual trajectory illumines the ideological journey that virtually all Spanish American political thinkers of the early nineteenth century were obliged to undertake. He began as a creole patriot and ended as something of a *philosophe*. Like other Jesuit exiles, he resented the philosophic historians' contemptuous dismissal of the New World and its inhabitants and strongly defended creole character and abilities. At the same time, he pictured colonial society as dwelling in hierarchical harmony, its peace disturbed only by the presence of European merchants and magistrates. But the more Viscardo compiled statistical data about trade, mining, and taxation in America, the more he came to construct a damning indictment of the Spanish colonial system. As his reading extended to encompass Adam Smith, so he fixed upon free and peaceful trade between nations as the chief promoter of liberty and prosperity. His famous *Letter* was written in the midst of his intellectual journey and presented an unstable combination of creole patriotism and Liberal philosophy. To be more precise, he combined ancestral rights based on conquest with universal "unalienable rights" common to all humanity. Moreover, by addressing himself to the American Spaniards, he acted as the spokesman of the creole nobility and failed to generate any concept of collective identity, be it of a republican *patria* or of a Peruvian nation. By the time he completed "Peace and Happiness," he had accepted the Enlightenment's critique of Hispanic civilization and condemned the Spanish monarchy as an intolerable despotism, more oppressive than its Ottoman counterpart. In this repudiation of the colonial epoch, Viscardo was the precursor of those nineteenth-century Liberals who dismissed the three hundred years of Spanish rule as a virtual Dark Age, in which despotism and superstition flourished, society vegetated, and the economy was exploited for the benefit of the metropolis.[71] In Viscardo's later writings, we can thus observe the crisis of creole patriotism and the birth of Spanish American Liberalism, which is to say, the abandonment of tradition and the espousal of Utopia.

NOTES

1. Teodoro Hampe Martínez, "Viscardo y Guzmán en Londres o los albores de la independencia hispano-americana (1791–1798)," D. A. Brading, Gustavo Gutiérrez, Manuel M. Marzal Fuentes, S. J., Gonzalo Portocarrero Maisch *et al., Juan Pablo Viscardo y Guzmán (1748–1798). El hombre y su tiempo,* 3 vols. (Lima: Fondo Editorial del Congreso del Perú, 1999), I, 167–88.

2. Robert Ernst, *Rufus King. American Federalist* (Chapel Hill, 1968), 264–70, 287–89.

3. For Miranda's comment and this English translation see Mario Rodríguez, *"William Burke" and Francisco de Miranda. The Word and the Deed in Spanish American Emancipation* (Lanham, Maryland, 1994), 159–61, 247.

4. *Ibid.,* p. 226. Note that Mill inserted this comment in his review of Juan Ignacio Molina's "History of Chile," published in *The Edinburgh Review,* July 1809.

5. Manuel de Mendiburu, *Diccionario histórico-biográfico del Perú,* 2d ed., 15 vols., ed. Evaristo San Cristóval (Lima, 1931–38). Note that the 4-vol. appendix inserted by the editor includes an account of Viscardo y Guzmán in part based on Rubén Vargas Ugarte, S. J., "Juan Pablo Viscardo y Guzmán 1747–1798," *Revista Histórica,* VIII (Lima, 1925), 5–18.

6. Rubén Vargas Ugarte, S. J., *La carta a los Españoles Americanos de don Juan Pablo Viscardo y Guzmán* (Lima, 1954); Miguel Batllori, S. J., *El abate Viscardo. Historia y mito de la intervención de los jesuitas en la independencia hispanoamericana* (Caracas, 1953), *passim.*

7. Merle E. Simmons, *Los escritos de Juan Pablo Viscardo y Guzmán. Precursor de la independencia hispanoamericana* (Caracas, 1983); "Viscardo y Guzmán's Two Sojourns in London. New Documentation," *Archivum Historicum Societatis Iesu* (hereafter cited as AHSI) LV (July–December 1986), 261–86; and "More about Viscardo y Guzmán's Sojourns in London," *AHSI,* LVIII (July–December, 1989), 121–88. The memoranda, essays, and letters discovered by Simmons were all written in French, save for some early letters in Italian; a convenient Spanish translation of all this material is to be found in Juan Pablo Viscardo y Guzmán, *Obra completa,* ed. Percy Cayo Córdova and César Pacheco Vélez, 2 vols. (Lima: Ediciones del Congreso del Perú, 1998). See also Merle E. Simmons, "Más en torno a las estadías de Viscardo en Londres," in

Brading, Gutiérrez, Marzal and Portocarrero, *Juan Pablo Viscardo y Guzmán*, I, 3–130.

8. For the 1781 letters see Viscardo y Guzmán, *Obra completa*, I, 5, 12–14.

9. *Ibid.*, I, 13–16.

10. See Miguel Batllori, S. J., *El Abate Viscardo*, 18–43; see p. 31 where his stipend is given at 372 *reales de vellón*, 20 of which were worth a silver peso.

11. Viscardo, *Obra completa*, I, 239–41.

12. *Ibid.*, I, 259–61.

13. Simmons, "Textus Inediti," *AHSI*, LVIII (1989) 142–56; see also James Hutton, *Selections from the Letters and Correspondence of Sir James Bland Burges, Bart., with some notices of His Life* (London, 1885), 130–32. I follow Simmons in calling him Bland Burges, although his contemporaries simply called him "Mr Burges"; his title, a baronetcy or hereditary knighthood, was given him on his retirement in October 1795. See also William Spence Robertson, *The Life of Miranda*, 2 vols. (Chapel Hill, N.C., 1929), I, 107–11.

14. Viscardo, *Obra completa*, I, 126.

15. Simmons, *Los escritos de Juan Pablo Viscardo y Guzmán*, 27–30.

16. Viscardo, *Obra completa*, I, 21, 26, 96–98, 113.

17. *Ibid.*, I, 23–24, 28–32, 95–104.

18. *Ibid.*, I, 56–57, 299.

19. *Ibid.*, I, 109–16; the citation from Montesquieu's *Spirit of the Laws* is from Bk. XXI, chap. 22, entitled, "Of the Riches which Spain Drew from America."

20. Viscardo, *Obra completa*, I, 120, 303–04.

21. David Patrick Geggus, *Slavery, War and Revolution. The British Occupation of Saint-Domingue 1793–98* (Oxford, 1982), 282–91. About 13,000 British soldiers died on Haiti, mainly as a result of yellow fever.

22. See Robertson, *Miranda*, I, 103, 169–70; for British expansion see Celia Wu Brading, *Generals and Diplomats. Great Britain and Peru 1820–1840* (Cambridge, 1991) 4–10; see also C. A. Bayly, *Imperial Meridian. The British Empire and the World 1780–1830* (London, 1989), 100–09.

23. H. S. Ferns, *Britain and Argentina in the Nineteenth Century* (Oxford, 1960), 18–49. See also Philip Henry Stanhope, *Notes of Conversations with the Duke of Wellington 1831–1851* (Oxford World Classics, 1938), 69, where, on reporting his dealing with Miranda, the Duke

added: "I always had a horror of revolutionizing any country for a political object. I always said, if they rise of themselves, well and good, but do not stir them up; it is a fearful responsibility...."

24. Melchor de Paz, "Diálogo sobre las sucesos varios acaecidos en este reyno del Perú," *Guerra separatista. Rebeliones de Indios en Sur América, la sublevación de Tupac Amaru,* ed. Luis Antonio Eguiguren, 2 vols. (Lima, 1952), *passim.*

25. Viscardo, *Obra completa,* I, 43–49; see also Scarlett O'Phelan Godoy, *Rebellion and Revolts in Eighteenth-Century Upper Peru* (Cologne, 1985), 161–275.

26. Viscardo, *Obra completa,* I, 49–50; Paz, "Diálogo," I, 405–06, 411.

27. Viscardo, *Obra completa,* I, 52–53; see also, John Leddy Phelan, *The People and the King. The Comunero Revolution in Colombia, 1781* (Madison, 1978), *passim.*

28. For this debate see Antonello Gerbi, *La disputa del Nuevo Mundo. Historia de una polémica 1750–1900* (Mexico, 1960), *passim;* also D. A. Brading, *The First America. The Spanish Monarchy, Creole Patriots and the Liberal State, 1492–1867* (Cambridge, 1991), 422–64. The critical texts on America were Guillaume Raynal, *Histoire philosophique et politique des établissements et du commerce des Européens dans les deux Indes,* in three revised editions, 1770, 1774, and 1781; William Robertson, *The History of America* (1777); and Jorge Juan and Antonio de Ulloa, *Relación histórica del viaje a la América meridional* (1748).

29. On these exiled Jesuits see Miguel Batllori, S. J., *La cultura hispano-italiana de los jesuitas expulsos* (Madrid, 1966), *passim;* both Clavijero and Molina published their works in Italian and were translated into English before being published in Spanish. Clavijero's original Spanish version was published as *Historia antigua de México,* ed. Mariano Cuevas, S. J. (Mexico: Editorial Porrúa, 1964). See also Juan Ignacio Molina *Geographical, Natural and Civil History of Chile* (London, 1782–87).

30. Viscardo, *Obra completa,* I, 62.

31. *Ibid.,* I, 63–71.

32. *Ibid.,* I, 68, 74–78.

33. *Ibid.,* I, 77–81

34. *Ibid.,* I, 81–84.

35. *Ibid.,* I, 85–88.

36. *Ibid.*, I, 54–56, 89–90; it was also Porlier who named Francisco Javier de Gamboa, a celebrated Mexican jurist, as regent of the *audiencia* of Mexico. See D. A. Brading, *Miners and Merchants in Bourbon Mexico 1763–1810* (Cambridge, 1971), 60–71, 103–05.

37. Viscardo, *Obra completa*, I, 91–94.

38. *Ibid.*, I, 291–96.

39. *Ibid.*, I, 205–06, 209, 213; see the 'De regimine principum' in *Aquinas. Selected Political Writings*, ed. A. P. D'Entreves (Oxford, 1954), 55–63.

40. *Ibid.*, I, 207–08.

41. Buenaventura de Salinas y Córdova, *Memorial de las historias del Nuevo Mundo, Perú*, ed. Luis E. Valcárcel and Warren L. Cook (Lima, 1957), 86–89, 162, 246, 275–77.

42. Viscardo, *Obra completa*, I, 211–13; see Brading, *The First America*, 540–51.

43. Viscardo, *Obra completa*, 209–10; see also El Inca Garcilaso de la Vega, *Historia general del Perú*, ed. Angel Rosenblat, 3 vols. (Buenos Aires, 1944), III, 243–51.

44. Viscardo, *Obra completa*, I, 210–14.

45. *Ibid.*, I, 211, 216; see also Thomas Paine, "Common Sense" (1776) in *The Thomas Paine Reader*, ed. Michael Foot and Isaac Kramnick (Penguin Books, London, 1987), 83, 86. Note that in Bk. XVIII of the third, 1781, edition of his *Histoire philosophique*, Raynal summarized Paine's *Common Sense*.

46. Viscardo, *Obra completa*, I, 217–18; *Thomas Paine Reader*, 65.

47. Emmanuel Joseph Sieyès, *What Is the Third Estate?*, ed. S. E. Finer (London, 1963), 59–62, 85.

48. Simmons, *Los escritos*, 151.

49. Eduardo Durnhofer (ed.), *Mariano Moreno Inédito. Sus Manuscritos, estudio preliminar de E. Williams Alzaga* (Buenos Aires, 1972), ix, 56, 73.

50. Servando Teresa de Mier, *Memoria político-instructiva enviada desde Filadelfia . . .* 2nd ed. (Mexico, 1822), 124.

51. Viscardo, *Obra completa*, I, 307; Hutton, *Bland Burges Papers*, 291–94. The Under-Secretary received a baronetcy and a pension of £1,500.

52. Montesquieu, *Spirit of the Laws*, Bk. XIII, ch. 17.

53. François de Salignac de la Mothe Fénelon, *Adventures de Télémaque*, ed. C. J. Dellile (London, 1854), Bk. XI, 244; not, as Viscardo gives, Bk. XIV.

54. Viscardo, *Obra completa,* I, 129–33. Note that in Bk. XIX of his 1781 edition, Raynal dwells extensively on the theme of universal peace and refers to "the virtuous prelate of Cambrai and the good Abbé de Saint Pierre" as the chief proponents of that cause.

55. Adam Smith, *The Wealth of Nations,* 2 vols. (London: Everyman, n.d.). In Bk. IV Smith gave his celebrated critique of mercantilism and colonial monopolies. See also Montesquieu, *Spirit of the Laws,* Bk. XX, ch. 2.

56. Fénelon, *Telémaque,* 186, 204, 214–15; Montesquieu, *Spirit of the Laws,* Bk. X, ch. 6–9.

57. Viscardo, *Obra completa,* I, 140–53.

58. Alejandro de Humboldt, *Ensayo político sobre el reino de la Nueva España* (Mexico: Editorial Porrúa, 1966), 422–28, 504–12, 551–53.

59. Viscardo, *Obra completa,* I, 140–74.

60. Jorge Larraín, *Theories of Development* (Cambridge: Polity Press, 1989), 85–107.

61. Viscardo, *Obra completa,* I, 178, 183–85; Benito Jerónimo Feijoo, *Teatro crítico universal,* 8th ed., 8 vols. (Madrid, 1753–55), IV, Discurso X, "Fábula de las Batuecas y Países imaginarios," 290–91.

62. Viscardo, *Obra completa,* I, 176–78, 181.

63. *Ibid.,* I, 188. Viscardo refers to Rousseau as simply "the author of *The Social Contract,*" citing Bk. III, ch. XII.

64. *Ibid.,* I, 185–93.

65. *Ibid.,* I, 219–23; on the Council of Pistoia and its "Jansenist" resolutions see Owen Chadwick, *The Popes and the European Revolution* (Oxford, 1991), 419–23.

66. Viscardo, *Obra completa,* I, 137, 179–80, 193.

67. *Ibid.,* I, 150.

68. *Ibid.,* I, 189–91, 201.

69. Brading, *The First America,* 540–44.

70. José de la Riva Agüero, "El Inca Garcilaso de la Vega," *Obras completas,* 13 vols. (Lima, 1962–96), II, 1–62.

71. It is no accident that whereas in his *Letter,* Viscardo addressed his compatriots as "American Spaniards," in "Peace and Happiness," he identified himself as a "Spanish American."

Juan Pablo Viscardo y Guzmán's

LETTER TO THE SPANISH AMERICANS

as it was published in

William Walton,
Present State of the Spanish Colonies
(London: Longman, Hurst,
Rees, Orme, and Brown, 1810),
Vol. II: Appendix D.

capital, is reckoned at one thousand two hundred and fifty dollars, or thereabouts, which in one year makes the sum of 450,000 dollars. But it is necessary to be understood, that among the Indians, very few use tobacco; among the Europeans, Creoles, Mullattoes and negroes, great numbers also do not use it.

Tobacco is a name, taken from the Cuban language. The Mexicans had two species of it, very different in the size of the plant, leaves, and in the figure of the flower, as well as in the colour of the seed. The smallest plant, which is the common one, was called by them picietl, and the largest quaujetl. The quaujetl grows as high as a moderate tree. Its flower is not divided into five parts, like that of the picietl, but only cut into six or seven angles. These plants vary much, according to clime, not only in the quality of the tobacco, but also in the size of the leaves and other circumstances, on which account several authors have multiplied the species.

D

LETTER TO THE SPANISH AMERICANS.

BROTHERS AND COUNTRYMEN,

OUR near approach to the fourth century, since the establishment of our ancestors in the New World*, is an occurrence too remarkable, not seriously to interest our attention. The discovery of so great a portion of the earth is, and ever will be, to mankind, the most memorable event in their annals; but, to us who are its inhabitants, and to our de-

* This letter was written apparently in 1791.

scendants, it is an object of the greatest importance. The New World is our country; its history is ours; and it is in the latter, that duty and interest oblige us to examine our present situation with its causes, in order to determine us, after mature deliberation, to espouse with courage, the part dictated by the most indispensable of duties towards ourselves and our successors.

Although our history for three centuries, as it relates to causes and effects the most worthy of our attention, be so uniform and plain, that one might abridge it into these four words—*ingratitude, injustice, slavery,* and *desolation;* it behoves us to study it a little more at large.

Our ancestors, in removing themselves to an immense distance from their native country, and in renouncing the support that belonged to them, as well as the protection which could no longer succour them in regions as distant as unknown; our ancestors, I say, in this state of natural independence, ventured to procure for themselves a new subsistence, by the most excessive fatigues, with the greatest dangers, and at their own expense.* The great success which crowned the efforts of the conquerors of America, gave them a right, which, without being the most just, was at least better founded than that of the ancient Goths of Spain, to appropriate to themselves the fruit of their valour and their labours: but the natural affection for their native country, led them to make her the most generous homage of their immense acquisitions, having no room to doubt that a gratuitous service of that importance, would secure them a proportionate gratitude; according to the custom in this century, of recompensing those who had contributed to extend the dominion of the nation.

These legitimate hopes having been frustrated, their de-

---

* Herrera says, that all the conquests were made at the expense of the conquerors, without the smallest cost to the government.

scendants, and those of other Spaniards, who successively emigrated to America, though we acknowledge the latter only as our country, and that the whole of our subsistence, as well as that of our posterity, is centered here; have respected, preserved, and cordially cherished the attachment of our ancestors to their former country: it is to her that we have sacrificed incalculable riches of every kind: it is for her alone that we have to this moment lavished our sweat; and it is for her besides, that on every occasion we have voluntarily shed our blood. Led by a blind enthusiasm, we have not considered that so much eagerness for a country to which we are strangers, to which we owe nothing, on which we do not depend, and of whom we expect nothing, becomes the worst treason to that in which we are born, and which furnishes nourishment to us and to our children; that our veneration for the affectionate sentiments of our ancestors, towards their former country, is the most decisive proof of the preference which we owe to our own; all that we have lavished upon Spain, has been snatched from ourselves and from our children, whilst our folly has been forging chains for us, which, if we do not break in time, no other resource remains to us, than to bear patiently this ignominious slavery.

If our present condition were as hopeless as it is afflicting, it would be an act of compassion to hide it from your view: but having in our hands the most certain remedy, let us unveil this frightful picture, and consider it by the light of truth. She informs us, that every law which opposes itself to the general good of those for whom it is made, is an act of tyranny; and that to exact observance to it, is enacting slavery; that a law which would directly tend to undermine the foundation of the national prosperity, would be monstrous beyond expression. Besides, it is evident, that the people whom they would rob of their personal liberty, and of the disposal of their property, whilst all other nations have at all times unanimously judged in similar circumstances that their vital interest was to extend them ;—that this same people would find themselves reduced to a state of vassalage, such as was imposed on enemies in the frenzy of victory.

These incontestable principles being admitted, let us see how they apply to our situation reciprocally with that of Spain. An immense empire, by us acquired, with treasures which surpass all imagination ; a glory and a power superior to all that was known to antiquity: these are our titles to the gratitude of Spain and of her government, and to their most distinguished protection. Yet our recompense has been such, that the most rigid justice would have hardly inflicted it as a punishment, if we had been guilty of the greatest crimes : she exiles us from the whole of the Old World, and cuts us off from the society to which we are connected by every tie ; adding to this unprecedented usurpation of our personal liberty, a second usurpation, no less important, that of our properties.

Since men began to unite in society for their mutual interest, we are the only people whom government has compelled to provide for our wants at the highest price possible ; and to part with our productions at the lowest price.—In order that this violence should have the most complete success, we have been cut off, as in a besieged town, from every channel through which we might have been able to obtain from other nations, at moderate prices and by fair exchanges, the commodities which we wanted. The imposts of government, the fees of officers, the avarice of the merchants empowered to exercise conjointly the most unbridled monopoly, —all bearing the same way, scarcity no longer left a choice to the purchaser ; and as this mercantile tyranny might force us to have recourse to our industry to supply our wants, the government took care to enchain it.

One cannot, without indignation, observe the effects of

this detestable plan of commerce ; and the details of it would be incredible, if those which have been given by persons of impartiality and worthy of belief, did not furnish the most decisive proofs for judging of the rest : without the occular testimony of Don Antonio Ulloa, it would be difficult to persuade Europeans, that the price of articles essentially necessary in all parts, such as iron and steel, was, in Quito, in time of peace, regularly beyond a *hundred dollars** for the quintal of iron, and about 150, for the quintal of steel ; the price of the first being in Europe only from five to six dollars, and that of the second in proportion : that in a port so celebrated as that of Carthagena, in the Indies,† and in like manner in time of peace, there has prevailed so great a scarcity of wine, that mass could be celebrated only in one church ; and that generally this scarcity and the exorbitant price, prevented the use of this beverage, rendered necessary above all others, by the insalubrity of the climate.

For the honour of humanity and of our nation, it is better to pass over in silence the horrors and the cruelties of another exclusive commerce (known in Peru, under the name of *repartimientos*) which the Corregidors and Alcades claimed to themselves, for the ruin of the unhappy Indians and Mestizos. What wonder then, if with so much gold and silver, with which we have nearly glutted the universe, we possess scarcely sufficient raiment to cover our nakedness. Of what use such a quantity of lands so fertile, if wanting the necessary instruments to till them ? It is besides useless for us to cultivate them beyond our consumption. Such benefits which nature bestows upon us, are in vain ; they accuse the tyranny which prevents us from drawing a profit from them, in partaking of them with other people.

* Voyage to South America, vol. ii   † Vol. i.

It seems, that without renouncing all sense of shame, no accession could be made to such great outrages.—The ingenious policy which, pretending our good, had stript us of liberty and of property, ought, one would think, to suggest, that it was necessary, at least, to leave us a shadow of honour, and some means for recovering us, and for preparing new resources. Thus it is, at least, that man grants nourishment and repose to the brutes that serve him. The economical administration of our interests might have consoled us for our other losses, and have procured also advantages to Spain. The interests of our country being no other than our own, their good or bad administration recoils necessarily upon ourselves ; and it is evident, that to us alone belongs the right of exercising it ; that we alone can fill its functions with reciprocal advantage to our country, and to ourselves.

What discontent did not the Spaniards shew, when some Flemish, subjects as well as they, and fellow countrymen of Charles the V. occupied some public employments in Spain ? What murmurs ? What expressions of dissatisfaction ? By how many remonstrances and insurrections did they not demand that those foreigners should be dismissed ? nor could their small number and the presence of the monarch, calm the general inquietude. The fear that the money of Spain should pass into another country, although belonging to the same monarchy, was the motive which made the Spaniards insist with the greater warmth upon their demand.

What a difference between this temporary situation of the Spaniards, and ours—which continues three centuries ! Deprived of all the advantages of government, we have experienced from it only the most horrible disorders and the greatest vices ; without the hope of ever obtaining, either an immediate protection, or a prompt justice, at the distance of from two to three thousand leagues, without the resource of objecting to them, we have been made the victims of the pride, the injustice, and the rapacity of ministers, as greedy at least as the favourites of Charles the V. Having no feeling for people with whom they were unacquainted, and whom they regarded as foreigners, they have sought solely to satisfy their cupidity; in perfect assurance that their iniquitous conduct would be concealed from the knowledge of the sovereign, or would remain unpunished. The sacrifice of our dearest interests to those of Spain, has been with them a patriotic claim, on which they all affected to pride themselves, in order to excuse the injuries with which they overwhelm us; but the misery into which Spain herself is fallen, proves that these men have never known the true interests of the nation, or that they have only sought to mask with this pretext their shameful proceedings, and the event has once more proved to a demonstration, that *injustice never produces solid advantages.*

To fill the measure of our humiliating slavery, indigence, covetousness and ambition, have always furnished to Spain, a host of adventurers ready to hurry to America; they arrive there determined to repay themselves amply, with our substance, for that which they have advanced to obtain their employments; they indemnify themselves for the abandoning their native country, for their hardships and dangers, by bringing with them all possible calamities; without ceasing, they revive those horrid scenes, which have made to disappear from the surface of the earth entire nations, whose sole crime has been weakness; they change the splendour of the grandest conquest, into an ignominious stain on the Spanish name.

Thus it is, that after having thriven in robbery covered with the name of commerce, in exactions of the government in return for its liberal benefits, and in rich places for the innumerable crowd of foreigners who, under different denominations, in Spain and in America, gorge themselves to satiety on our properties; the remaining part is the continual object of the snares of those proud tyrants; whose rapacity knows no other bounds, than those of insolence and the certainty of impunity.

Thus, whilst at court, in the armies, and in the tribunals of the monarchy, they lavish riches and honours upon foreigners of all nations, we alone are declared unworthy of them; we are declared incapable of filling, even in our own country, places which, in the strictest right, belong to us exclusively. Thus the hard-earned glory of our ancestors, is converted for us into an inheritance of infamy; and with our immense treasures, we have purchased only misery and bondage.

Let us survey our unhappy country all over, and we shall every where find the same desolation;—every where an avarice as excessive as it is insatiable;—every where the most abominable traffic of injustice and inhumanity, on the part of blood-suckers employed by government for our oppression. Let us consult our annals for three centuries; they discover to us the ingratitude and injustice of the Court of Spain, and its treachery in not fulfilling the engagements contracted at first with the great Columbus, and afterwards with the other conquerors, who gave to it the empire of the New World, on conditions solemnly stipulated; we shall see the offspring of those magnanimous men branded with scorn, and pursued by the hatred which has calumniated, persecuted, and ruined them. After these simple particulars, should the spirit of persecution be doubted, which has at all times signalized itself against the Spanish Americans; read only what the authentic *Inca Garcilaso de la Vega* has written in the second volume of his Commentaries, book 8, chap. 17.

When the viceroy, Don Francisco de Toledo, that fero-

cious hypocrite, put to death the sole direct heir to the empire of Peru, in order to secure the possession of that unhappy country to Spain, in the process which he instituted
against the young and innocent *Inca Tupac Amaru*,
among the false crimes with which this prince was charged,
" They accuse," says Garcilaso, " those who were born in
this country, of Indian mothers and Spanish fathers, the
conquerors of this empire; they alleged that they were se-
cretly agreed with Tupac Amaru and other Incas, to excite
a rebellion in the kingdom, to favour the discontent of
those who were born of the royal blood of the Incas, or
whose mothers were the daughters, nieces, or cousins-ger-
man of the family of the Incas, and the Spanish fathers,
and first conquerors, who had acquired so much reputation: that the former were so little considered, that neither
the natural right of the mothers, nor the great services and
merits of the fathers, procured them any advantage, but
the whole were distributed amongst the relations and friends
of the governors: that themselves alone remained exposed
to the horrors of hunger, or reduced to the dreadful alter-
native of living on charity, or becoming highwaymen, and
ending their miserable existence on the gallows. These ac-
cusations being preferred against the sons of the Spaniards
born of Indian women, they were all seized, and those
amongst them who were of the age of twenty and upwards,
capable of carrying arms, and then dwelling at Cusco, were
imprisoned: some were put to the torture, to force them to
confess that of which there were neither proofs nor appear-
ances. In the midst of these furious and tyrannical proceedings, an Indian woman, whose son was condemned to
the rack, came to the prison, and raising her voice, ex-
claimed: ' My son, since they have condemned you to the
torture, endure it courageously, like a man of honour; accuse none falsely, and God will give you strength to bear

it; He will compensate you for the dangers and the troubles which your father and his companions have endured to render this country Christian, and to introduce its inhabitants into the bosom of the church.' This magnanimous exhortation, uttered with all the vehemence of which this mother was capable, made the greatest impression upon the mind of the viceroy; she diverted him from his design of putting those unhappy persons to death; however they were not acquitted, but were condemned to a slower death, in exiling them into different parts of the New World—some were even sent to Spain."

Such were the first fruits which the offspring of the discoverers of the New World, received from the gratitude of Spain; when the remembrance of the deserts of their ancestors was still recent. The viceroy, this sanguinary monster, then appeared the author of all those wrongs; but we deceive ourselves respecting the sentiments of the Court, if we believe that it did not participate in these excesses; in our days it has thought proper to renew them in every part of America, in snatching from her a greater number of her children, without seeking even to disguise its inhumanity: they have been deported even as far as Italy. After having cast them upon a country a stranger to her dominion, and having renounced them as subjects, the Court of Spain, by a contradiction, by an unheard-of refinement of cruelty, and with that unrelenting rage which the fear alone of sacrificing innocence inspires in tyrants, has reserved to itself the right of unceasingly persecuting and oppressing them: death has already delivered the most part of these exiles from the calamities which have accompanied them to the tomb; the others drag on a miserable existence, and furnish a new proof of that cruelty of character, which has been such a reproach to the Spanish nation, though really this reproach ought to fall only on the despotism of her government. *

Three whole centuries, during which this government has, without interruption, held the same conduct with regard to us, afford complete proof of a meditated plan, to sacrifice us intirely to the interests and the convenience of Spain; but above all to the passions of her ministers. It is not less evident, that notwithstanding the multiplied efforts of a false and iniquitous policy, our establishments have acquired such consistence, that Montesquieu, that sublime genius, has said, " The Indies and Spain are two powers under one master, but the Indies are the principal; Spain is only the accessory. In vain policy pretends to bring back the principal to the accessory; the Indies however draw Spain to them." † This means, in another sense, that reasons for tyrannizing over us are every day increasing: like a perverse guardian, who is accustomed to live in pride and opulence at the expense of his ward, the Court of Spain sees with the greatest fear the moment approach, which nature, reason, and justice have prescribed, for emancipating us from such an oppressive guardianship.

The void and confusion which the annihilation of this prodigal administration of our wealth will produce, are not the only motives which engage the Court of Spain, in perpetuating our minority, to increase the weight of our chains: the despotism which, with our treasures, she exercises over the ruins of Spanish liberty, would receive a mortal blow from our independence; and it is the business of ambition to prevent it by every effort.

The claim of the Court of Spain to a passive obedience to its arbitrary laws, is founded principally on the ignorance

* In the year 1789, there were living in Italy five hundred Ex-Jesuits, natives of Spanish America.

† Liv. xxi. chap. 22.

which she has taken care to keep up and encourage, especially with respect to the indefeasible rights of man, and the indispensable duties of every government; she succeeded in persuading the common people, that it is a crime to reason on subjects which concern vitally every individual, and consequently that it is always a duty, to extinguish the precious torch which the Creator has put into our hand to enlighten and conduct us. In spite of the progress of so fatal a doctrine, every page of Spanish history deposes against its truth and legitimacy.

After the memorable epoch of the arbitrary power and injustice of the last Gothic kings, which brought on the ruin of their empire and of the Spanish nation, our ancestors, in re-establishing the kingdom and its government, thought only of guarding against the absolute power to which our kings have always aspired. With this design, they concentred the supremacy of justice, and the legislative powers of peace, war, subsidies, and the granting of monies, in the *Cortes* which represented the different classes of the nation, and were to be the depositaries and guardians of the rights of the people.

To this solid barrier the people of Arragon added the celebrated magistrate, named *El Justicia*, to protect them against every violence and oppression, as well as to repress the abusive power of the kings. In the preamble of one of their laws, the people of Arragon say, according to *Jerome Blanca*, in his Commentaries, page 751, " That the sterility of their country and the poverty of its inhabitants are such, that if liberty did not distinguish them from other nations, the people would forsake their native country, and would seek establishments in a more fertile region." And to the end that the king may never forget the source whence he derived his sovereignty, the *Justicia*, in the solemn ceremony of coronation, addressed him with the following

VOL. II.   z

words: " Nos, que valemos quanto vos, os hacemos neus-
tro rey y senór, con tal que guardeïs neustros fueros y liber-
tades, y sino, no;" * as is related by the celebrated Antonio
Perez, secretary to Philip the II. It was therefore a
fundamental article of the constitution of Arragon, that,
if the king violated the rights and privileges of the people,
the people had a right to disown him for their sovereign,
and to elect another in his place, even of the *Pagan* religion, according to the same Jerome Blanca.

It is to this noble spirit of liberty, that our ancestors
have been indebted for the energy which made them achieve
such grand enterprises, and which, in the midst of so many
burdensome wars, made the nation flourish, and filled her
with a prosperity equal to that of England at present, and
Holland formerly; but since the kings have overleaped the
limits which the constitution of Castile and that of Arragon
had prescribed, the decline of Spain has been as rapid
as the extraordinary power acquired, or rather usurped by
the sovereigns; and this sufficiently proves, that absolute
authority, with which arbitrary power always blends itself,
is the ruin of states.

The re-union of the kingdoms of Castile and Arragon,
as well as the great states which, at the same time, fell to the
kings of Spain, together with the treasures of the Indies,
gave to the crown of Spain an unforeseen preponderance,
which became so powerful, that in a very little time, it
overthrew all the barriers raised by the prudence of our
forefathers, for assuring the liberty of their posterity: the
royal authority, like the sea overflowing its boundaries, in-
undated the whole monarchy, and the will of the king and
his ministers became the general law.

Despotic power once so solidly established, even the sha-

* We, who are as good as you, make you our King and Lord, provided
that you preserve our rights and liberty, and if not, no.

dow of the ancient *Cortes* existed no more; there remained to the natural, civil, and religious rights of the Spaniards, no other safeguard, than the will and pleasure of the ministers, or the ancient formalities of justice, called *vias juridicas*; these last have sometimes been successfully opposed to the oppression of innocence, without however preventing the verification of the old proverb: *Where kings will, the laws give way*.

A happy invention furnished, at last, the most fruitful means for removing those troublesome restraints. The supreme economical power, and *the motives reserved in the royal bosom*, (expressions which cannot fail to astonish posterity) discovering at last the vanity of all the reveries of mankind about the eternal principles of justice, on the rights and duties of nature and of society, have suddenly displayed their irresistible force on more than *five thousand* Spanish citizens. *

Observe, that these citizens were united in one body, which, to its social rights in quality of members of the nation, joined the honour of public esteem, merited by services no less useful, than important. †

Omitting the reflections suggested by all the circumstances of so strange a proceeding, and leaving apart the

* In the year 1786, there were in Italy more than three thousand Spanish Ex-jesuits—the remainder of those five thousand unfortunate persons: having for the whole of their subsistence only a pension of two paolis per day, a pittance scarcely sufficient to maintain a servant.

† "*Paraguay* (says Montesquieu) can furnish us another example. It has been imputed as a crime to the company of the Jesuits, that they were fond of command; but it will ever be a sublime appendage of authority, to use it to make a people more happy.

"It will be ever glorious for them to have been the first to spread in those countries the light of religion, joined with that of humanity. In repairing the devastations of the Spaniards, she has begun to heal one of the deepest wounds which mankind has received.

z 2

unhappy victims of this barbarous outrage, we will consider it only with regard to the whole Spanish nation.

The preservation of the natural rights, and especially of the liberty and security of persons and property, is undoubtedly the foundation-stone of every human society, under whatever form it may be constituted: it is therefore the indispensable duty of every society, or of the government which represents it, not only to respect, but still further effectually to protect the rights of every individual.

Applying these principles to the present subject, it is clear that five thousand Spanish citizens, whom to that moment the public opinion had had no reason to suspect of any crime, have been stript by the government of all their rights, without any accusation, without even the forms of justice, and in the most arbitrary manner. The government has solemnly violated the public safety, and until it gives a satisfactory account of the motives which have made it act so despotically, there is no individual who, instead of the protection which is his due, may not have a like oppression to fear, particularly as his individual weakness exposes him more than a numerous body, and which, for many reasons, interested the whole nation. A fear so serious and well founded, naturally excluded every idea of safety; the government, guilty of having destroyed it in the aggregate, has converted into instruments of oppression and ruin, the means entrusted to it for the protection and security of individuals.

"A lively sentiment which this society entertains for what they call honour, their zeal for a religion which humbles much more those to whom it is preached than those who preach it, have made them undertake great things, in which they have been successful. They have collected from the woods people before dispersed; they have given them a secure subsistence, and have clad them; and even this increase to society and stimulus to industry alone, would entitle them to the gratitude of posterity." Esp. des Lois, liv. iv. chap. 6.

If government believe itself in duty bound to revive public security, and the confidence of the nation, in the integrity of its administration, it ought to manifest in the clearest juridical manner, the justice of its cruel procedure towards the above-mentioned five thousand individuals; and, in the mean time, it is obliged to confess the crime which it has committed towards the nation, in transgressing an indispensable duty, and in exercising a merciless tyranny.

But should the government think itself superior to this justification, what difference is there between its subjects and a flock of sheep, of which the capricious owner can dispose or make sacrifice at will? The base and timid silence of the Spaniards on this horrible procedure, justifies the discernment of the ministry, which has dared to undertake without fear an enterprise as difficult as it was unjust. And if it happens in political diseases as in those of the human body, that the symptoms are never so dangerous as when the patient seems insensible to the violence of his distemper, truly the Spanish nation, in its present condition, has some consolation for its misfortunes.

The progress of this great revolution in the constitution and government of Spain, which we have just sketched, and which has been handed down to us, coincides with our national history; let us now proceed to examine the influence we ourselves may hope or dread from its results.

Whilst the known causes of any evil gradually grow worse, it would be folly to expect the opposite good. We have seen the ingratitude, the injustice, and the tyranny with which the Spanish government oppressed us from the foundation of our colonies, that is to say, when it was very far from possessing the absolute and arbitrary power to which it has since arrived; now that it knows no other rules than its will, and that it is accustomed to consider our property as an estate which belongs to it, all its study consists in increasing it at our expense, in always giving the colour of utility to the *mother country*, to the infamous sacrifice of all our rights and of our dearest interests. This logic is that of highwaymen; it justifies the usurpation of the goods of another, by the utility which arises from them to the usurper.

The expulsion and the ruin of the Jesuits had, according to every appearance, no other motives than the report of their riches : the latter being exhausted, the government, without pity for the disastrous situation to which it has reduced us, wished to aggravate it still further by its new imposts, particularly in South America, where, in 1780, it cost Peru so much blood. We should groan still under this new oppression, if the first sparks of an indignation too long repressed, had not forced our tyrants to desist from their extortions. *Generous Americans of the new kingdom of Grenada!* If Spanish America owes you the noble example of intrepidity, which ought always to be opposed to tyranny, and the new lustre added to its glory, it is in the annals of humanity that we shall see engraven in immortal characters, that your arms protected our countrymen, the poor Indians, and that your deputies stipulated for their interests with the same successful zeal as for your own. May your magnanimous conduct become a useful lesson to the whole human race!

The ministry is far from renouncing its projects of swallowing up the miserable remains of our property; but disconcerted by the unexpected resistance which it experienced at Zipaquira, it has changed the means of arriving at its aim, and adopting, when least expected, a system contrary to that which its mistrustful policy had invariably observed, it has resolved to furnish arms to the Spanish Americans, to instruct them in the military discipline; it hopes, without doubt, to obtain from the regular American troops, the

same assistance which it finds in the bayonets of Spain, to
enforce obedience; but thanks to Heaven, the corruption
of the principles of humanity and of morality, is not arrived
at its full measure amongst us; never shall we become the
barbarous instruments of tyranny, and sooner than stain
ourselves with the least drop of the blood of our harmless
brothers, we will shed all our own, in defence of our rights
and of our common interests.

A powerful navy ready to convey to us all the horrors of
destruction, is the other means which our past resistance
suggests to tyranny; *this is the necessary support of government, and of the preservation of the Indies:* it is or-
dained by the decree of the 8th of July, 1787, that the
*rents of the Indies (the article of tobacco excepted) pre-
pare funds sufficient for defraying the half or the third of
the enormous expenses which the royal navy requires.*

Our settlements on the continent of the New World,
even in their state of infancy, and when the power of Spain
was in its greatest decline, have always been sheltered from
every hostile invasion; and our strength being now much
more considerable, it is clear that the increase of the land
and sea forces is, in respect to us, an expense as enormous
as useless to our defence; thus this formal declaration, announced with so much candour, seems only to indicate
that the paternal vigilance of the government for our prosperity, of which to this moment it has afforded us the
sweets, intends to give us new proofs of its zeal and its attachment.*   In consulting the ideas of justice, which one
may suppose to belong to every government, we would be
tempted to believe, that the funds which we ought to fur-

* As often as the Spanish government announces to us a benefit, one re-
members what the executioner said to the son of Philip the II., in putting
the knife to his throat, " Silence, silence, my Lord Don Carlos, this is all for
your good."

nish for defraying the enormous expenses of the royal navy, are destined to protect our commerce and to multiply our riches, so that our ports, like those of Spain, are to be free to all nations ; and that we shall be at liberty ourselves, to visit the most distant regions, there to sell and buy at the first hand : then our treasures will no more issue forth like torrents never to return, but circulating amongst ourselves, they will perpetually increase by industry.

We should the more indulge in those flattering hopes, as they are conformable to the system of union and equality, of which the government, in the royal decree, desires the establishment between us and the Spaniards of Europe. What a vast field will then open, for obtaining at court, in the armies, and in the tribunals of the monarchy, the honours and the riches which have been so constantly refused us ! The European Spaniards having had to the present moment the exclusive possession of all these advantages, it is but just that government, to establish this perfect equality, begin by placing them on the same footing in which we have been so long a time. We should then alone frequent the ports of Spain, and become the masters of her commerce, of her riches and of her destiny; we cannot doubt but that the Spaniards, witnessing our moderation, will quietly submit to this new arrangement ; the system of equality, and our example justify it wonderfully.

What would Spain and her government say, if we should seriously insist upon the execution of this fine system; and why insult us so cruelly in speaking of union and equality ? Yes, equality and union, like that of the animals in the fable, in which Spain reserves to herself the part of the lion. Is it only after three centuries, that the possessions of the New World, our country, is our due, and that we ought to hear of the hope of becoming equal to the Spaniards of Europe ? And why, and by what title, should we be deprived of this equality? Alas! it is by our blind, our base submission to all the outrages of the government that we have deserved, that it has conceived of us an idea so contemptuous and insulting. Dear brothers and countrymen! if amongst us there be a person who does not know and feel his wrongs more sensibly than I should know how to express them, the ardour which manifests itself in your soul, the great examples of your ancestors and your eager courage, prescribe to you the resolution that alone suits with the honour which you have inherited, which you cherish, and which you value beyond every thing. This resolution, the government of Spain has itself pointed out to us, in constantly considering you as a people distinct from the European Spaniards, and this distinction imposes on you the most ignominious slavery. Let us agree on our part to be a different people; let us renounce the ridiculous system of union and equality with our masters and our tyrants; let us renounce a government, whose excessive distance prevents us from procuring even in part, the advantages which every man ought to expect from the society to which he is attached; this government, which in place of performing its indispensable duty, in protecting the liberty and safety of our persons and properties, has shewn the greatest eagerness to destroy them; and which, in place of endeavouring to render us happy, continues to overwhelm us with all kinds of calamity. Since the rights and duties of government and of the subjects are reciprocal, Spain has been first in transgressing all her duties towards us; she also has first broken those feeble bonds which would have been able to attach and retain us.

Nature has separated us from Spain by immense seas: a son who should find himself at a similar distance from his father, would without doubt be a fool, if in the conduct of his least concerns, he always waited the decision of his father. The son is set free by natural right: and ought a numerous people, who do not depend for any thing on another people, of whom they have no need, to be subjected to them like the vilest slaves?

The local distance which proclaims our natural independence is still less than that of interests. We have essential need of a government which would be in the midst of us, for the distribution of benefits,—the object of the social union. To depend on a government removed two or three thousand leagues, is equal to our renouncing those benefits; and this is the interest of the Court of Spain, which aspires to give us laws, to domineer over our commerce, our industry, our wealth, and our persons, only to sacrifice them to its ambition, its pride and its avarice.

In fine, under whatever aspect our dependence on Spain may be viewed, we shall see that all our duties oblige us to put an end to it. We owe it in gratitude to our ancestors, who were far from lavishing their blood and sweat, in order that the theatre of their glory and of their labours should become that of our miserable slavery. We owe it to ourselves, by the indispensable obligation of preserving the natural rights received from our Creator, those precious rights which we have not the power to alienate, and which cannot, under any pretext, be ravished from us without crime. Can man renounce his reason, or can it now be torn from him by force? Personal liberty belongs to him, not less essentially than reason. The free enjoyment of those same rights, is the inestimable inheritance which we ought to transmit to our posterity.

It would be a blasphemy to imagine, that the Supreme Benefactor of man has permitted the discovery of the New World, merely that a small number of imbecile knaves might always be at liberty to desolate it; and that they should incessantly have the odious pleasure of stripping millions of men, who have given them no cause of complaint, of essential rights received from his divine hand; to imagine that his eternal wisdom wished to deprive the remainder of mankind of the immense advantages which, in the order of nature, so great an event ought to procure for them, and to condemn them to wish with a groan, that the New World had remained for ever unknown. This blasphemy, however, is put into practice by the right which Spain arrogates over America, and human malice has perverted the natural course of the bounties of the Almighty, without regard to what was due to our particular interests on account of the defence of the country. We are bound, as far as lies in our power, to fulfil the hopes of which hitherto they have frustrated mankind. Let us throw open a second time America to all our brother inhabitants of this globe, from whence ingratitude, injustice, and the most senseless avarice have exiled us; the recompense will not be less to us than to them.

The many regions in Europe, which the crown of Spain has been obliged to renounce, such as the kingdom of Portugal, placed within the compass of Spain, and the celebrated republic of the United Provinces, which shook off its iron yoke, tell us that a continent infinitely larger than Spain, richer, more powerful, and more populous, ought not to depend on that kingdom, when it finds itself at such a distance; and still less, when it is reduced to the hardest slavery.

The valour with which the English colonies of America have fought for the liberty, which they gloriously enjoy, covers our indolence with shame; we have yielded to them the palm with which they have been the first to crown the New World by their sovereign independence. Add the eagerness of the Courts of Spain and of France to assist the cause of the English Americans; it accuses us of insensibility; let at least the feelings of honour be roused—by outrages which have endured for three hundred years.

We have no longer any pretext to cover our resignation; and if we longer bear the oppressions which overwhelm us, it will be said with reason, that our cowardice has merited them; our descendants will load us with imprecations, when, biting in vain the curb of slavery—of a slavery which they shall have inherited, they will remember the moment in which to be free, we had only to will it.

That moment is arrived, let us seize it with all the feelings of pious gratitude; and if our efforts be ever so faint, well-ordered liberty, that precious gift of heaven, accompanied by every virtue, and followed by prosperity, will commence her reign in the New World, and tyranny will be speedily exterminated.

Animated by so great and just a motive, we may, with confidence address ourselves to the eternal principle of order and justice, to implore with our humble prayers the divine assistance, and in the hope of being favourably heard, to console us for any misfortunes that may ensue.

This glorious triumph will be complete, and will cost little to humanity; the weakness of the only enemy who has an interest in opposing it, does not permit him to employ open force, which would accelerate his entire ruin. His principal support is in the riches which he draws from us; withhold those from him, and let them be applied to our own defence, we shall render his rage impotent. Our cause, besides is so just, so favourable to mankind, that there is but little chance of finding amongst other nations, one who will load itself with the infamy of combatting us; or who, renouncing its personal interests, will venture to oppose the general wishes in favour of our liberty. The wise and virtuous Spaniard, who groans in silence under the oppression of his country, will himself applaud our undertaking. We shall see the national glory revive in an immense empire, become the secret asylum of all Spaniards, who, besides the brotherly hospitality which they have always experienced, will be able moreover to breathe there freely under the laws of reason and justice.

May that day, the happiest that shall have ever shone, I do not say upon America, but the entire surface of the globe, arrive speedily ! That day, when to the horrors of tyranny, of oppression and of cruelty, shall succeed the reign of reason, of justice, and of humanity; when the tears, the distresses, and the groans of eighteen millions of men, shall give way to mutual confidence, to the most open satisfaction, and to the pure enjoyment of the benefits of the Creator, whose sacred name shall no more serve as a mask to robberies, fraud,' and ferocity; when the odious barriers, which the most besotted selfishness, in sacrificing its true interests to the detestable pleasure of preventing the prosperity of others, in opposition to the happiness of all mankind, shall be overturned, what an agreeable and affecting spectacle will the fertile shores of America present, covered with men from all nations exchanging the productions of their country against ours ! how many from among them, flying oppression or misery, will come to enrich us by their industry and their knowledge, and to repair our exhausted population ! Thus would America unite the extremities of the earth ; and her inhabitants, united by a common interest, would form one GREAT FAMILY OF BROTHERS.

E

REVOLUCION DE CARACAS.

La revolucion de Caracas rompió en la ciudad de Venezuela en 19 de Abril proximo pasado. La tropa tomó el

BIBLIOGRAPHICAL NOTE

by Burton Van Name Edwards

H ABENT SUA FATA LIBELLI—every book has its own story, and the purpose of this brief bibliographical sketch is to make more precise the relationship between Viscardo's original essay and the English translation of 1810 presented here in a facsimile edition.[1] In the first printed version of 1799, the editor, the famous Precursor, Francisco de Miranda, cryptically claimed that "this writing was apparently completed in 1791."[2] Thanks to the discovery a few years ago by Merle Simmons of a series of letters written by Viscardo to James Bland Burges, the Undersecretary of State in the British Foreign Office in the early 1790s, we now have confirmation that Viscardo's work was, in fact, completed in 1791.[3]

But more importantly, this letter to Bland Burges of September 15, 1791, makes it clear that the original version of Viscardo's *Lettre*, published in French, was in fact first composed in Spanish and subsequently translated by the author himself into French.[4] Until Simmons's discovery in 1989, scholars, including Simmons himself, had concluded, based on the fact that all the manuscripts of Viscardo's works were in French, that this native Spanish speaker had, contrary to all expectations, originally composed his works in French.[5] Unfortunately, the original manuscript, in Spanish, no longer exists. The earliest state of Viscardo's text then must be reconstructed from the comparison of the manuscript in the Bland Burges papers at the Bodleian Library and that at the New-York Historical Society, which, at Viscardo's death in 1798, had come into the possession of Rufus King, then American ambassador to Great Britain. Ultimately, Viscardo's papers, including a manuscript of the *Lettre aux Espagnols-Américains,* were deposited in the New-York Historical Society with the rest of the Rufus King papers. When Simmons compared the two manuscripts, he found that corrections in the New York manuscript were embodied in the text of the Bland Burges manuscript, while the Bland Burges text omitted a lengthy passage drawn from Garcilaso de la Vega. Accordingly, Simmons concluded that the New York manuscript was the exemplar for the text given to Bland Burges, although the language of the Bodleian manuscript was more polished than that in the Rufus King papers.[6]

Soon after Viscardo's death, King lent the manuscript of the *Lettre* to Francisco de Miranda, who prepared the text for publication. In the following year, Viscardo's *Lettre aux Espagnols-Américains* appeared in London with the false imprint of Philadelphia—a time-honored device to disguise the true origins of potentially dangerous texts.[7] By his own admission, Miranda considerably revised Viscardo's original text.[8] By comparing the 1799 printed text with the King manuscript, Simmons concluded that, while Miranda made many changes to Viscardo's text, the fundamental ideas were in no way altered. The most significant changes were the addition of a long list of ex-Jesuits exiled from Spanish America and living in Italy as well as a lengthy passage from Bartolomé de las Casas.[9]

Two years later, Miranda supervised the translation of Viscardo's *Lettre* into Spanish. Despite the many errors introduced by the non-Spanish speaking printer, this Spanish version faithfully reproduced the earlier French version while carefully preserving the changes and additions Miranda had contributed to Viscardo's original text.[10] Needless to say, Viscardo's text was to have its greatest influence in this translation and the Spanish version was published a number of times between 1810 and 1822.[11]

On January 1, 1808, Francisco de Miranda returned to London to seek the support of the British government for his Venezuelan independence projects. Undoubtedly, among his earliest contacts was the mysterious "William Burke," who was about to publish a second treatise in favor of British intervention in South America.[12] Within a short period of time, "William Burke" [i.e., probably James Mill] published a relatively brief (91 pages) discussion of British policy in South America, responding to the humiliating British defeat at Buenos Aires.[13] But in June, 1808, "Burke's" treatise was republished in a second edition, with the inclusion of a translation into English for the first time of Viscardo's *Lettre aux Espagnoles-Américains*.[14] We can only infer that from the time of their first meeting, Mill and Miranda had been working on this English translation and that it was published as soon as possible. A close reading of the English text proves that it was based on the 1799 French edition and not on the later Spanish translation and that some of Miranda's additions to the two earlier printed editions, i.e., the lengthy list of ex-Jesuits, had been removed.

This English translation of Viscardo's letter was the foundation stone of the "paper Assault" that was to consume much of Miranda's and Mill's energy during the next two years. In January 1809, Mill published an unsigned review of the "Philadelphie" edition of Viscardo's letter in the *Edinburgh Review,* containing several pages of direct quotations from Viscardo's *Letter* and a paraphrase of many of the treatise's arguments favoring the emancipation of Spanish America.[15] Mill continued his polemical endeavors in the July issue of the *Edinburgh Review* with a lengthy review of Giovanni Ignazio Molina's *Natural History of Chile* and his *Civil History of Chile.*[16] This concerted attempt to sway British foreign policy towards active intervention on behalf of the emancipation of South America was to culminate in

1810 with the publication of *South American emancipation. Documents, historical and explanatory, showing the designs which have been in progress, and the exertions made by General Miranda, for the attainment of that object during the last twenty-five years,* which reprinted the *Edinburgh Review* essay by Mill that had incorporated so many of Viscardo's thoughts.[17]

William Walton was responsible for the second English translation of Viscardo's treatise, which is reprinted in the present volume.[18] Walton had traveled extensively in Spanish America as a young man, returning to England only in 1809 after a long stay in Santo Domingo.[19] He was to have a long career attacking British policy in respect to South America, and he found the polemical tone of Viscardo's *Letter* to his liking. Accordingly he appended a slightly edited version of the 1808 "Burke" translation to his massive treatise, *Present state of the Spanish colonies,* published in 1810.[20] Walton made very few changes in the Burke translation. Since it was an appendix, the title page was dropped, along with Miranda's introductory note.[21] Miranda's list of Jesuits, which had been dramatically edited in the Burke translation, was not even mentioned by Walton. Finally, Walton also dropped the long quotation from Las Casas, which Miranda had inserted on the final page of Viscardo's treatise.[22] Otherwise, Walton was content to change a word here and there every few paragraphs, but in general his text is virtually identical to "Burke's." Ironically, since Walton's translation definitively eliminated two of the longest passages added to Viscardo by Miranda in 1799, this second English translation in a certain sense is the most faithful reproduction of Viscardo's original text. Within a decade of the publication of Walton's translation, the various countries of Spanish America began their move to independence, without the assistance of Britain, and consequently Viscardo's treatise lost its relevance to contemporary affairs. But now, more than 175 years later, its passion and polemical clarity still ring out clearly, even in the English translation.

1. Probably influenced by the spelling of our author's name on the title page of the influential work of R. Vargas Ugarte, *La Carta a los españoles americanos de don Juan Pablo Vizcardo y Guzmán* (Lima: Editorial del cimp, [1954]) (some subsequent bibliographies even silently altered the spelling of Ugarte's title page), American libraries have followed suit and adopted the "Vizcardo" spelling. Ugarte was aware that contemporaries such as Miranda spelled the name "Viscardo," but citing our author's baptismal certificate and the preferences of his Peruvian ancestors, he opted for the "Vizcardo" spelling (see Ugarte, p. xivn). However, recent scholarship, citing our author's preference in the extant manuscripts, has almost unanimously spelled the name "Viscardo."

2. Juan Pablo Viscardo y Guzmán, *Lettre aux Espagnols-Américains.* A Philadelphie [i.e. London], MDCCXCXIX[sic][1799], p. in: Cet écrit fut apparement fait en 1791.

3. Merle E. Simmons, "More about Viscardo y Guzmán's Sojourns in London," *Archivum Historicum Societatis Iesu* 58 (1989), 121–88, esp. 164–74.

4. The title of the Bland Burges copy reads: "Lettre aux Espagnols Americains, traduite de l'originale Espagnol." See Simmons, "More about Viscardo," 165n.

5. Merle E. Simmons, *Los escritos de Juan Pablo Viscardo y Guzmán. Precursor de la Independencia Hispanoamericana.* (Caracas: Universidad Católica Andrés Bello Instituto de Investigaciones Históricas, 1983), esp. p. 29.

6. Simmons, "More about Viscardo," 172–74.

7. Earlier scholarship had accepted the Philadelphia imprint as true. See, for example, William Spence Robertson, *The Life of Miranda* (Chapel Hill: University of North Carolina Press, 1929), Vol. I, 195–96. Vargas Ugarte, *La Carta,* 73–74, argues for Philadelphia as the place of printing, but recent scholarship has suggested that the 1799 French edition was printed by the same press in London that produced the 1801 Spanish translation. See Juan Pablo Viscardo y Guzmán, *Obra Completa. Biblioteca Clásicos del Perú,* 4 (Lima: Banco de Crédito del Perú, [1988]), 444–45. My own casual examination of the two editions confirms this hypothesis, that the same press produced both versions, since the type for page numbers and other type devices are very similar, while the size of the text block is almost identical.

8. Archivo de Miranda, XV, pp. 409–10.

9. Simmons, *Los escritos*, 87–91. On pages 363–84 of this work, Simmons reprints the 1799 edition, showing all the variations with the New York/King manuscript.

10. Juan Pablo Viscardo y Guzmán, *Carta Derijida à los Españoles Americanos. Por uno de sus compatriotas.* Impreso de Londres por P. Boyle, Vine Street, Piccadilly. 1801. For a reprint, see Viscardo, *Obra completa*, 271–314.

11. Viscardo, *Obra completa*, 446–48.

12. For the identification of "William Burke" as James Mill, see Mario Rodríguez, *"William Burke" and Francisco de Miranda: the Word and the Deed in Spanish America's Emancipation* (Lanham (MD): University Press of America, 1994), esp. Ch. 4: William Burke: Front and Center!

13. Rodríguez summarizes this text on pp. 72–82 of *"William Burke."* The title of this work was: *Additional Reasons for our Immediately Emancipating Spanish America* (London: J. Ridgway, 1808).

14. This edition of "Burke's" *Additional Reasons* differs from the first by the insertion of an edition statement on the title page, a brief preface, and an appendix of some forty pages containing Viscardo's letter and some documents. These documents relate to Miranda's Venezuelan expedition of 1806.

15. "Art. II. Lettre aux Espagnols-Americain. Par un de leurs Compatriots. A Philadelphie. 8vo. pp. 42," *The Edinburgh Review,* no. xxvi [26] (January 1809), 277–311.

16. Rodríguez, 225–37.

17. J. M. Antepara, who appears as the author on the title page, merely edited Miranda's papers. The imprint for the work is London: Printed by R. Juigné, 1810.

18. Some bibliographies suggest that Viscardo's letter was published in the United States in 1809. See for example, Juan Pablo Viscardo y Guzmán, *Obra completa: Edición de Homenaje del Congreso de la República y de la Comisión Nacional encargada de los Actos commemorativos del 250° Aniversario del Nacimiento de Juan Pablo Viscardo y Guzmán, Precursor de la Independencia americana* (Lima: Ediciones del Congreso del Perù, 1998), T. II, 446. But if one reads the letter of Samuel C. London of Oct. 17, 1809, cited there from the original in the Archivo del General Miranda (La Habana: Editorial Lex, 1950), T. XXIII, 117–20, it will be clear that London is alluding to the *Edinburgh Review* version of Viscardo's work.

19. "Walton, William" in *Dictionary of National Biography* (New York: Macmillan, 1899), vol. 59, 280–81.

20. William Walton, *Present state of the Spanish colonies; including a particular report of Hispañola, or the Spanish part of Santo Domingo* (London: Printed for Longman, Hurst, Rees, Orme, and Brown, 1810). 2 vols. Viscardo's "Letter to the Spanish Americans" appears as an appendix to vol. II, pp. 326–49.

21. Miranda's introductory note, as it appears in Burke's translation is as follows: "The following interesting Letter, from an American Spaniard to his countrymen, is translated from a French copy printed conformably with the manuscript, written by the author himself; who died in London in the month of February 1798. The Translator begs, at this highly interesting moment, to present to the British nation this valuable little tract; which came to his hands only a short time since, and which does equal honour to the writer, as an enlightened patriot, politician, and Christian."

"The reader will perceive in the perspicuous and animated language of this South American divine, when speaking of the slavery and sufferings of his country, an expanded liberality, a comprehensiveness of views, and a just and noble indignation against the oppressors of his native land, not unworthy of the best of times or friends of their country, even in nations famed for THEIR liberty and civilization in Europe: and if those be the sentiments of some of the clergy of Spanish America, whom it is too much the vulgar custom unjustly to stigmatize for their bigotry, may it not be reasonable to expect, that a corresponding spirit of liberality and patriotism, has also found its way amongst the laity, the melioration of whose condition more imperiously demanded a change?—That it has done so, is evident from the circumstances now taking place on the South American Continent: and I have no doubt a very short time will convince us, that the progress of this alteration in the minds of the Spanish American people, has been more rapid and complete, than many individuals in this country are prepared or inclined to believe."

22. Miranda added and Burke translated into English the following passage from Bartolomé de las Casas: "What just motive could the Spanish Government have in declaring war against the Indians (says the virtuous Las Casas) who had never done them a wrong, or injustice in any manner! They had never seen or known them: they were not come down to ravage their lands: they never have made the profession

of Christianity like the Moors of the kingdom of Grenada, &c.—Still less could they reproach the Indians with being the declared enemies of our faith, or of leaving no stone unturned to destroy by open persecutions or by secret persuasions, in forcing the Christians to renounce their faith to oblige them to become idolaters. The laws divine and human have never permitted to make war on nations, under the pretext of establishing Christian faith in them; unless it is meant to be maintained, that the evangelical law, full of charity, of mildness and of humanity, ought to be introduced into the world by force, like the laws of Mahomet.

"There are no places in the world where men and other animals multiply as in the Indies; because the air which we respire in that country is mild and favourable to propagation. But the Spaniards have discovered the secret of entirely depopulating countries filled with an infinite multitude of men and women: they have unjustly massacred them, in order to seize the gold and silver which they possessed; they have caused others to perish, by making them toil to excess, or by obliging them to carry heavy loads for the distance of a hundred or two hundred leagues: so that, for the sake of riches, they sacrificed the life of the Indians. We advance nothing that is not very true, and yet we do not relate half the things which we have seen." D. B. de Las Casas, *la Decouverte des Indes.* Paris, 1697.

This book was designed and set in Caslon
by Gilbert Design Associates, Providence, Rhode Island,
and printed by The Stinehour Press, Lunenburg, Vermont
on Mohawk Superfine paper.
It was bound by Acme Bookbinding Company, Inc.,
Charlestown, Massachusetts.

1,250 copies for the John Carter Brown Library
March 2002